MARIJUANA A SHORT HISTORY

A SHORT HISTORY

making. During that time, government, society, popular culture, and the public have evolved on a number of issues surrounding marijuana—often in very different directions.

This plant has been farmed out to the fringes of society by prohibition, vilification, racialization, and legitimate concerns about its consequences for public health and public safety. Yet marijuana is a pervasive part of society—garnering attention from government, serving as a symbol of societal protest, filling the lyrics of songs and the scripts of movies, and becoming the most widely used substance deemed illegal by the U.S. government. America has experimented with marijuana in a multitude of ways, with a variety of outcomes and consequences. The following pages provide a gateway to a greater understanding of marijuana's history in the United States.

THIS BOOK HAS FIVE PARTS. Cannabis is a chemically rich and diverse plant that can be used for a variety of purposes. Part I explains the plant's botanical profile and provides a description not only of the products made from different types of cannabis but, most significant, the scientific understanding of how chemicals in cannabis interact with the human body. When grown for drug production, once harvested and processed, marijuana is transformed into a menu of "delivery systems"—ways to get it into the human body that have changed over time.

Part II covers the history of marijuana-related government policy from 1906, the administration of Teddy Roosevelt, to the early 1990s, the presidency of George H. W. Bush. It examines the myriad ways the federal government sought to regulate drugs generally, and marijuana specifically. During this period, the U.S. government's marijuana focus shifted from product safety to revenue production to restriction and eventually to total prohibition of the drug and draconian sanctions associated with its production, distribution, sale, and use. This historical overview includes the War on Drugs and the racialization of U.S. drug policy. These developments set the scene for more recent marijuana policy in the United States: pushback against a nearly century-long regime of control by the federal government.

Part III looks at how public opinion on marijuana policy has changed. It charts the evolution not just in poll results, but in the manner in which popular culture has treated the drug. From *Reefer Madness* to Bob Marley's album *Kaya* (*kaya* is Jamaican slang for "weed") to Dave Chappelle's movie *Half Baked*, the cultural treatment of cannabis has both prodded and been a reaction to public views. In addition, I examine the evolution of political officials' resistance to or embrace of marijuana use and what their experiences mean as society and public policy change with regard to marijuana acceptance.

Part IV examines how marijuana has blossomed and evolved into a serious public policy issue. It profiles some of the early efforts to reform marijuana laws including decriminalization at the city level and early efforts to legalize at the state level. Here I discuss legislative and ballot initiative efforts, the professionalization and mainstreaming of the movement itself, and international drug reform efforts.

Part V looks toward the future. The current political dynamics at the state and federal levels in the United States are instructive, and I apply the historical record as a context to understand how reform may advance. In this part I look at both the policy benefits and consequences of marijuana reform and discuss how current public policy challenges can and should be resolved in order to create a regulatory, administrative, and market regime that is consistent, credible, and reliable.

PART I **A WEED BY ANY OTHER NAME**

ONE CANNABIS AS PLANT AND PRODUCT

MARIJUANA IS SUBJECT to numerous misconceptions and confusion. There is disagreement on some basic issues, such as how the cannabis plant grows, how it interacts with the body, where it comes from, and how long it has been in use. Before jumping into a discussion of marijuana policy, it is important to dispel these misconceptions regarding the plant and its products.

Some popular misconceptions include that marijuana is easy to grow, that it can grow under almost any conditions, and that it's pretty much the same everywhere. You grow it, pluck its flowers, dry them, wrap them in rolling paper, and smoke it, and there you have it, your weed, or pot, or Mary Jane. In reality the cannabis plant is biologically complex, and the production of marijuana is not as simple as many people believe.

In addition, marijuana has changed over time with innovations in growing, harvesting, and generating products. Marijuana is no longer something you pack into a bowl, roll in a joint, smoke in a bong, or lace into some brownies. It is now a diverse consumer product available in many forms.

THE CANNABIS PLANT   Members of the *Cannabis* genus are leafy, flowering plants that are native to Central Asia but have been transported and grown throughout the world. The plant has been around for millions of years in some form and has been used by humans for at least 5,000 years.[1] It tends to be robust and grows effectively in both natural and controlled agricultural settings, and has been described as "a rapidly growing dioecious (male and female reproductive organs on different plants), wind pollinated, annual herb that in some plant selections can reach heights of 20 feet."[2] Historically botanists have disagreed as to the number of species in the genus *Cannabis,* but there is now general agreement that the three principal *Cannabis* species are *C. sativa*, *C. indica*, and *C. ruderalis*. Each has its own distinct look, chemical characteristics, and uses.

Cannabis plants grow quickly and can be harvested on accelerated timelines, particularly in controlled agricultural settings. Depending on the species and strain, cannabis has five, seven, or sometimes nine leaves that are dark green and sometimes purple-hued. The plant produces a flower at the tip of the stem and the base of the leaves. The flowers—or bud—have the most powerful concentration of the chemicals that produce an effect on the brain; they are harvested to produce the drug marijuana, particularly when it is to be taken in the most traditional way: smoked. However, other parts of the plant also contain some of the same chemical components, called cannabinoids, that can be psychoactive or nonpsychoactive. So all of the plant's parts are harvested in commercial production in order to extract cannabinoids.

The drug marijuana is not the only product produced from cannabis. Hemp fibers are produced from specific cannabis plants that are low in cannabis's main psychoactive chemical, tetrahydrocannabinol (THC). Hemp stalks can produce strong, fibrous material used for clothing, lines and sails for ships, and other purposes. Its seeds are used as a protein-rich food, and from those seeds oils are extracted that can be used for cooking or other uses. Hemp can also be purposed for use as a biofuel. During certain periods of American history, hemp growth was encouraged or even required because of its versatility and usefulness, particularly in wartime.

Different cannabis varieties grow better under different conditions. Some prefer warmer climates whereas others can survive in colder conditions farther north. One of the most critical aspects of growing cannabis is the light cycle. Different varieties have different requirements for light and dark in order to maximize and facilitate growth:

> If vegetative growth conditions are favorable, the stem will increase in height by two inches per day when exposed to the long daylight of summer. While some selections of Cannabis are day-neutral (flower under any day length), most are classified as short-day plants

(they need a long dark period, usually fourteen hours or more) and shift from vegetative to generative (reproductive) growth upon exposure to short daylight periods.[3]

This sensitivity to light and dark signals two important facts about cultivating cannabis. First, it is not as easy to cultivate cannabis as the moniker "weed" would suggest. Despite cannabis's robustness, it can also be sensitive to growing conditions. Second, because certain varieties of cannabis can require extended periods of darkness to maximize the growth and generative phases, the plant lends itself to indoor-grow environments in which periods of light and dark can be strictly controlled.

Water is another area where cannabis has specific requirements. The amount of water provided and the water's acidity levels and nutrient balances are critical. Although cannabis can grow under a variety of conditions, if a grower wishes to maximize a plant's productivity and ensure that its chemical composition is consistent and true to its strain (an important aspect of cannabis grown commercially for the production of marijuana), success requires research, care, frequent attention, and horticultural and agricultural know-how.

CANNABIS SPECIES   The two most common species of cannabis are *sativa* and *indica*, typically used in the production of marijuana. Strains of these two species are rich in THC and are used for both medicinal and recreational marijuana. A third, lesser-known, species, *ruderalis,* tends to have much lower levels of THC. Although cannabis can be grown as a "pure" species—*sativa*-only or *indica*-only—an entire cottage industry has emerged around marijuana genetics. This involves the cross-pollination or cross-breeding of different strains and even different species of cannabis to produce new hybrid strains. Much of the genetic diversification is driven by the desire to satisfy consumer tastes, as different combinations offer the user different experiences.

For instance, it is commonly said that "*sativa* gets you high; *indica* gets you stoned." This reflects the user experience whereby *sativa* strains produce a euphoric feeling whereas *indica* strains are more mellow and relaxing. The combinations of different species, different strains, or both create many types of chemical combinations and lead to a wide array of experiences, feelings, and responses. Strains have been developed to increase a user's energy, stimulate the appetite, relax the body, give someone the giggles, suppress the appetite, or help the user focus.

The development of new strains and thus new experiences sometimes happens by accident, but it also emerges from intensive efforts around plant genetics. Research in cannabis genetics occurs in laboratory settings—the scientific pursuit of the perfect high—and also in less formal settings. Individuals who pride themselves as experts or pioneers in this endeavor—working around the world, but particularly in Canada, California, Colorado, and the Netherlands—are producing some of the most sought-after strains.

The three species also differ physically. *Indica* plants tend to be shorter, stockier plants, whereas *sativa* plants can grow to significant heights. The stems of *sativas* are a bit more firm, so hemp is derived from these plants.

Ruderalis plants tend to be the smallest of the cannabis group in height and girth. This species also tends to be less potent because of years of natural cross-breeding in its native Central Russia.[4] It functions more like a wild cannabis, whereas *indica*, *sativa*, and their hybrids are usually produced under very controlled environments.

The diverse characteristics of cannabis plants and their specific needs as an agricultural product suggest how much time and thought must be committed to ensure cultivation expertise. I have provided only a glimpse of the technical requirements of growing marijuana. In "Cannabis Grow Revolution," Danny Danko details the numerous considerations that a cannabis cultivator faces.[5] He explores hydroponic growing methods, soil requirements, fertilization, pest control, and the choice over indoor and outdoor cultivation. Danko details why cultivating cannabis properly to produce high-quality marijuana is an art.

CANNABINOIDS Few people are familiar with the word "cannabinoid," but every person who has used marijuana has experienced the effects of cannabinoids. Cannabinoids are chemical compounds found in the cannabis plant. These chemicals interact with the human body in ways that cause specific sets of reactions. Whatever one feels when using marijuana—excited, mellow, funny, confident, paranoid, hungry, pain-free—one feels this way because cannabinoids are having an effect on the brain.

Cannabis plants contain dozens of these chemicals, but just one or two are commonly known: tetrahydrocannabinol (THC) and cannabidiol (CBD). THC and CBD are prominent in commercialized marijuana: dispensaries in marijuana-legal states often list the percentages of each in a product. THC is the psychoactive component that most users want and that contributes to making the user feel high. CBD, on the other hand, is often associated with medical marijuana, especially treatment for conditions such as epilepsy. CBD has been found to have anti-convulsive and anti-spastic properties that can relax muscles and regulate the brain in ways that can prevent minor and major seizure events. CBD acts in a variety of ways, also possessing anti-inflammatory and other properties. The precise combination of THC, CBD, and the more than sixty other identified cannabinoids in marijuana work together to create the type of effect one gets from using marijuana.

The way cannabinoids interact with the human body is quite interesting and is actually a modern medical discovery. In 1988 a pharmacology researcher named William Devane and his colleagues discovered something interesting: the human body is built to smoke pot. Well, maybe not exactly. But it is built to be receptive to the effects of pot. There are receptors in the brain and elsewhere that are sensitive to cannabinoids and produce, or hinder, chemical responses in reaction to the presence of cannabinoids. This system was dubbed the endocannabinoid system. What's more, subsequent researchers identified "endogenous cannabinoids," molecules the human body produces naturally that interact with endocannabinoid receptors; when external cannabinoids such as THC or CBD from the cannabis plant are present, they work with the endogenous molecules and the body's own receptors to produce a variety of effects within the human body.[6]

It is not fully known how the human body reacts to or benefits from these chemicals. Research shows that the endocannabinoid system can produce neuroprotective responses that can assist in dealing with seizures or brain injuries. It can assist in blunting pain receptors. The chemicals have an impact on the biological processes that cause anxiety. Additional and ongoing research, needed now more than ever, will help the scientific community better understand cannabinoids and the responses of the endocannabinoid system. Such research will become more likely as more and more responsible, innovative entrepreneurs are allowed to operate within a strict regulatory environment.

MARIJUANA STRENGTH   The "strength" of marijuana is measured by how rapidly the body takes up the chemicals and the user feels their effects. The "strength" of marijuana is an interesting concept. Anyone who has used marijuana multiple times has likely encountered "strong stuff." Typically, that refers to marijuana that gets you high faster or has a stronger effect. That is typically measured by the level of THC, the main psychoactive chemical compound in marijuana. Higher levels of THC can cause more intense effects or speed up the desired effect.

Marijuana, particularly smoked marijuana, has a self-regulating effect because the onset of the psychoactive experience is so rapid that the smoker is quickly satisfied and is not motivated to continue to smoke. This differs from the common experience with alcohol, where large quantities can be consumed before the full effects are felt, at which point one may have drunk too much.

The rise of marijuana edibles, however, particularly in marijuana-legal states, has posed challenges for both self-regulation and the consistent experiences of users. Marijuana edibles come in many countless forms including cookies, brownies, candies, granola, salad dressing, and even pasta sauce. Edibles on the commercial market often come with significant amounts of THC because one unit—a single candy bar or cookie—may contain multiple servings. In Colorado, for example, a standard edible serving has 10mg of THC. Some products for purchase contain five or ten servings, amounting to 50mg or 100mg of THC.

The onset of edible marijuana's psychoactive effects is dramatically slower than that of smoked marijuana— sometimes thirty minutes to an hour or more. Because of this delay, users—especially a naïve user—can overconsume, believing the edible is weak. This can cause unpleasant effects and a very intense high when all the THC is absorbed. This has come to be called the "Maureen Dowd effect," after the *New York Times* columnist who famously and irresponsibly overconsumed marijuana edibles in Colorado, had a bad reaction, and wrote about it in her column, blaming the products rather than the consumer.[7] In fact, in this case, the product is not "stronger." Instead, the product is overconsumed.

Some argue that marijuana has gotten much stronger over time, but this claim is controversial. A researcher at the University of Mississippi, Dr. Mahmoud ElSohly, is one of the nation's leading experts on the cannabis plant and the effects of marijuana—he runs the only marijuana grow operation approved by the federal government. Part of his job is also to test the strength of marijuana seized by federal law enforcement agents. He notes that since

1970, the THC content of seized marijuana has increased from an average of around 3 percent to around 7 to 8 percent in the late 2000s.[8] Recent evidence suggests this figure now averages about 13 percent THC.[9]

ElSohly's findings do not tell the whole story about changes in the strength of marijuana, however. His research tells us only about the strength of *seized* marijuana. The reality is that as states have legalized marijuana, cannabis genetics have taken off and entrepreneurs have invested in development and become more innovative. And consumer tastes for stronger marijuana have had genuine market effects—legal marijuana varieties can be quite strong. Street weed in 2016 may be slightly stronger than it was in 1970, but the commercial product can be quite a bit stronger. In marijuana-legal states, some strains have a THC content higher than 20 percent. The black market just has to deliver marijuana; the legal market must meet consumer demand.

DELIVERY SYSTEMS: THE NEW WORLD
OF MARIJUANA PRODUCTS
If you have used marijuana from an illegal source and have never bought it in a legal medical or recreational market, your familiarity with marijuana probably extends to smoking it and eating brownies laced with pot. You may be unfamiliar with just how many different marijuana products are out there. The variety now available is a real testament to American entrepreneurialism and innovation.

Most people are introduced to marijuana by smoking it, and smoking remains the most common "delivery system," or method of consumption. By harvesting flowers from the cannabis plant, grinding them, and burning them, users can inhale the THC-rich smoke and be fast on their way to getting high. The vehicle for smoking can vary and include a joint, a blunt, a pipe, a bong, among others. The effects of marijuana are felt quite quickly, as the lungs absorb the cannabinoids in the smoke and quickly transfer them to the bloodstream and then to the brain. There the endocannabinoid system works its magic.

There are some drawbacks to smoking. First, it can cause irritation of the throat. Anyone who makes a first attempt to smoke pot or inhales their first hit in a long time can feel the smoke burning the bronchial passages. Second, smoking pot produces secondhand smoke, which may or may not cause a contact high, but in either case may be undesirable to those affected. Third, long-term use of smoked marijuana is associated with bronchial irritation and an increased likelihood of respiratory infections (most medical evidence suggests that smoking pot does not increase the incidence of pulmonary cancer). Fourth, advocates of medical marijuana are concerned that the Food and Drug Administration will never approve smoked marijuana as a pharmaceutical because smoking itself is harmful to health.

Despite all of these issues, marijuana flower remains the most popular marijuana product and smoking remains the most widely used method.

Edibles are another common delivery vehicle for marijuana. Users producing edibles at home infuse food products with marijuana. Typically, marijuana flower is boiled or simmered in a fat (butter or oil, as the chemical components are fat soluble) and that infused fat is used as part of a recipe. Brownies, cookies, and other sweets are a popular way to eat marijuana, but the legal market has produced a wider variety of premade edibles, as mentioned above.

Essentially, a cannabis culinary professional can infuse just about anything you want to eat with THC for you. The market for edibles has grown dramatically. The flavor can be a delight, eating these products can be discreet (even making it possible to covertly consume in public where public use is illegal), and there are none of the secondhand effects produced by smoking. For marijuana tourists staying in hotels that ban smoking, edibles provide an avenue to enjoy marijuana without having to hand over a cleaning fee to the clerk at the front desk.

Edibles could be misused (overconsumed), but seasoned consumers largely avoid such trouble. Another legitimate concern with edibles is accidental ingestion by children or by adults who do not know a food product is infused with THC. Despite those risks, edible marijuana products are becoming a significant portion of the consumer market.

In addition to products designed for smoking and eating are a significant number of marijuana-based technologies that, while not invented recently, are new to a lot of American consumers. One that is rapidly growing in popularity is "vaping," which is similar to smoking but involves the ingestion of vaporized marijuana. There is no smoke, no burning of the product. It is less harsh on the lungs and has no secondhand effects. Vaping usually involves a mechanized, often battery-powered device that looks like a pen or (ironically) a Breathalyzer, that can use either flower or oil extracts of cannabis. The contents are heated to a high enough temperature to bond with water vapor, but not high enough to combust. The burning process involved in smoking can reduce the amount of THC and other cannabinoids that can be ingested. More of the cannabinoids are preserved by avoiding combustion and using vaporization as a means of ingestion. In marijuana-legal states vaping is growing in popularity because it remains a bit more discreet than smoking, can be ingested more slowly with reduced loss of product compared to burning, and allows the user to avoid the lingering scent in the air and on clothing characteristic of smoking.

Similar to smoking or vaping is "dabbing." Dabbing is consumed using dabs—ultra-concentrated extracts from marijuana. Usually a waxy resin or oil that is very high in THC content is either burned or vaporized, emitting a potent blast of inhalable product. Dabbing requires a "dab rig," which often looks like a less sophisticated bong. Using it requires heating a surface, such as a ceramic or metal plate, and touching the dab to that heated surface (holding it with a nail or some long tweezer) while the user inhales. The user need not consume much and the effect is fast and powerful. The benefit, particularly for medical patients seeking pain relief, is the rapid, potent onset of the effects. However, some people report that dabs are more potent than they wish. Others, even in a recreational setting, prefer the dabbing experience to standard vaping or smoking.

Then there are tinctures of marijuana. Tinctures are typically cannabinoid-laden oils that are administered orally via a dropper. Tinctures can be used recreationally by including significant levels of THC or they can be used medicinally using THC, CBD, or some balanced combination of the two. In this case cannabinoids such as (most commonly) CBD, THC, tetrahydrocannabolic acid (THCA), cannabinol (CBN), and others are extracted from plant parts, purified, and often bonded with oil. Many of these cannabinoids are associated with the effective treatment of multiple conditions, but the anti-convulsive properties of cannabinoids make tinctures more common in the treatment of epilepsy-related conditions, especially in children, as well as of multiple sclerosis, amyotrophic lateral sclerosis (ALS, also known as Lou Gehrig's disease), and other such illnesses.

Several other vehicles of delivery are more often associated with medical than recreational uses of cannabis. Cannabis in capsule form is common in medical-marijuana-legal states where use is heavily regulated and pharmaceutical in nature and only a limited number of products is allowed. The technique does preserve some of the optics of medicine for patients seeking a discreet means of taking the substance their doctors recommend.

Some patients use a variety of patches that transfer cannabinoids into the system, also in discreet ways, including transdermal patches. In addition to discretion, transdermal patches confer the benefit of a steady time release of cannabinoids into the system.

Another delivery means is the sublingual strip, which patients place behind the lip or under the tongue. Though this method does not provide the same time release that a transdermal strip does, it provides patients an additional discreet vehicle of delivery. Transdermal patches and sublingual strips can provide relief for patients who suffer from nausea and who prefer not to smoke and whose nausea symptoms eliminate edibles as an option.

An entire volume would be needed to cover all of the cannabis-delivery products available for sale in the states that have some form of legalized marijuana. For medical or therapeutic purposes, ointments, creams, lip balms, salves, massage oils, moisturizers, and hundreds of other products exist. The development of ever more products is driven by both producers and consumers. Producers want to make "the next big thing" in marijuana—the product that strikes gold, goes viral, and makes its inventor rich. For consumers, the goal is basic: to get cannabinoids into their system in the most desirable and effective way possible. Those forces together have created a booming corporate industry that is pumping billions of legal dollars into the U.S. economy annually.

WHAT'S IN A NAME? Throughout this book, I use the terms "cannabis" and "marijuana" somewhat interchangeably. At times, I use "cannabis" to describe the plant (*Cannabis sativa* or *C. indica*) and "marijuana" to describe the harvest of the cannabis plant and the consumer products derived from it. That choice is a personal one; the distinction has no formal basis—although I have read and heard others assert that the distinction should be maintained.

Those choices, however, mask a controversy that I feel must be addressed. Many individuals, especially those in the cannabis advocacy community, refuse to use the word "marijuana" and prefer to use "cannabis" exclusively. The level of commitment to that terminology became apparent to me at a 2015 conference on the topic where a speaker said he preferred "not to spell cannabis with an *m*." At first I didn't get what he was saying, but then I realized he meant he refused to utter the word "marijuana."

The argument made by some who are opposed to the word "marijuana" is that it is a historically racialized term, promoted by scholars, government officials, and the media to turn public opinion against both the substance and entire groups of people. This statement is not far-fetched. Historically in the United States, words, music, products, and behaviors have been labeled in ways that explicitly or implicitly injected race into their usage. That racialization of language has affected African Americans and immigrant groups from Mexico, the rest of Latin America, Asia, Ireland, Italy, eastern Europe, and elsewhere.

Originally, "marijuana" (also spelled "marihuana") comes from Mexican Spanish, and in the early twentieth century it was used as a colloquial or slang term to describe cannabis. However, during and especially after the Spanish-American War, American resentment toward Mexicans and Mexican immigrants exploded. Tensions, particularly along the southern border of the United States, were quite high and the response was predictable: media stories vilified entire groups of people, negative portrayals of Mexicans appeared in entertainment venues, and race-baiting language seeped into the rhetoric of politicians and government officials. Martin Lee notes in the prologue of *Smoke Signals* that the word "marijuana . . . was popularized in the United States during the 1930s by advocates of prohibition who sought to exploit prejudice against despised minority groups, especially Mexican immigrants."[10]

As Mexican immigrants streamed across the border, Americans were increasingly uncomfortable with their new neighbors. It was easy to heap blame on the new immigrants for a variety of problems in society, including crime. And one stereotype was "Mexicans using marihuana." Media outlets began reporting crimes committed by Mexican immigrants using that image. The change in language around the term "marijuana" was so stark that, a National Public Radio report noted, "This disparity between 'cannabis' mentions pre-1900 and 'marihuana' references post-1900 is wildly jarring. It's almost as though the papers are describing two different drugs."[11]

This war of words was reflected not only in the public news media but also in official language. Government officials also gladly participated. Harry Anslinger was one such government official. As the head of the Bureau of Narcotics, he served as the nation's top drug cop from 1930 to 1962. His passion for drug prohibition was fundamentalist. His racism was no secret. His words were laden with fear, vilification, and xenophobia.

In speeches around the country, testimony to Congress, and articles that he published in both the popular press and more serious journals, Anslinger made it his mission to outlaw drugs, and he wholeheartedly embraced "marihuana" for its "Mexican-ness" and its ability to serve the ends he sought. In one essay, Anslinger tells readers about marijuana's entry into American society and its effects: "Marijuana was introduced into the United States from Mexico, and swept across America with incredible speed. It began with the whispering of vendors in the Southwest that marijuana would perform miracles for those who smoked it. . . . They were not told that addicts may often develop delirious rage during which they are temporarily and violently insane; that this insanity may take the form of a desire for self-destruction or a persecution complex to be satisfied only by the commission of some heinous crime."[12] Anslinger goes on to list multiple brutal crimes, attributing each to the use of the scary weed from Mexico.

In addition to Anslinger, local police chiefs and district attorneys played an important role not just in pushing the word "marijuana" into common parlance but in slathering it in a coating a racial resentment. In 1931 the district attorney of Orleans Parish in Louisiana, Eugene Stanley, published an article in the *American Journal of Political Science* about the different groups that historically had been "marihuana" users, including Mexicans, Indians, Persians (a group called Assassins), Malays, and others.[13] Stanley goes on to note, "The underworld has been quick to realize the value of this drug in subjugating the will of human derelicts to that of a master mind. Its use sweeps away all restraint, and to its influence may be attributed many of our present day crimes. . . . It has been indulged in by criminals so as to relieve themselves from the natural restraint which might deter them from the commission of criminal acts."[14]

These efforts by government officials are clear in their intent: to link marijuana to unknown, mysterious, or feared groups from other parts of the world, and to link the usage of marijuana to lawlessness and serious criminal offenses. In effect, marijuana—not cannabis or hemp—was a scourge on society, brought to us by all the people we fear or should fear. The race baiting is obvious, and "marijuana" became the preferred term for those spewing xenophobic rhetoric.

The advocacy community's rejection of the term "marijuana" is based on a legitimate interpretation of the history of the term's usage. Other authors and speakers who prefer to use "cannabis" are perfectly within their right. I understand fully their position, continue to respect the concerns of those who despise the term, and know this note will do little to justify my position or convince some of the legitimacy of my choice. I have chosen to use "marijuana" in this book—even in the title—because of contemporary uses of the term. It is mainstream; it is standard; it is the term Americans use almost universally when discussing cannabis and its products. There may well be people who still use the term as a means of invoking racialized language, but most Americans do not.

PART II **THE GOVERNMENT STEPS IN**

TWO EARLY REGULATION AND A NEW (DRUG) DEAL

DURING THE LAST DECADES of the nineteenth century, Progressives sought to institute reforms to empower the federal government to regulate commerce in ways that protected workers, consumers, and the public. Progressive regulation grew to touch many facets of American life such as the temperance movement and the push for workers' rights. It also shaped early efforts to regulate food and drugs.

The American medical system in the nineteenth century was a largely unregulated one in which doctors were often poorly trained, and little standardization was applied to the elixirs the medical community used to treat conditions and diseases. Patient safety was threatened. The medical community and state governments began to consider ways in which the quality and delivery of medicine and medical products could be improved.

THE GOVERNMENT STEPS IN AS REGULATOR   In 1906 Congress passed the Federal Food and Drug Act, one of the nation's first efforts to regulate and standardize commercial drugs, food, and other products. The focus was on the branding, packaging, and adulteration of such products. The law, empowering the U.S. Department of Agriculture's Bureau of Chemistry to test and regulate substances, had a clear impact on marijuana. "Drugs" in the law are substances "defined in the United States Pharmacopeia or National Formulary." According to the website of the U.S. Pharmacopeial Convention, "The United States Pharmacopeia and The National Formulary (USP–NF) is a book of public pharmacopeial standards for chemical and biological drug substances, dosage forms, compounded preparations, excipients, medical devices, and dietary supplements."[1] The USP-NF is the Holy Bible for pharmacists; until 1942, marijuana had its own chapter and verse.

The Federal Food and Drug Act did not outlaw marijuana, nor even tax it. Essentially it allowed the Agriculture Department to put standards in place to ensure its safe use. In fact, as long as the USP-NF included marijuana, the substance was legal and regulated under the act. However, the act did mark the expansion of the federal government's regulatory power into a new arena—an expansion that would eventually be approved by the U.S. Supreme Court. It put the federal government in the business of controlling drugs, a power that would only grow over time.

In fact, shortly thereafter Congress passed what came to be known as the Opium Exclusion Act of 1909 in response to racially motivated disputes with Chinese immigrants in the West. This act banned the import of opium and its derivatives into the United States. Over time the banning of opium imports would be expanded to other drugs.

In 1914 Congress passed the Harrison Act, named after its chief sponsor, Representative Francis Burton Harrison (D-N.Y.), which created a prescription registry and imposed a special tax of one dollar per year for anyone manufacturing, distributing, or dispensing opium and cocaine.[2] It allowed the government to keep an account of prescriptions written for such substances and prescribed criminal penalties for doctors who violated the act by dispensing or possessing such substances without permission or without paying requisite taxes. In fact, doctors were prosecuted under this law. Physicians undertook efforts to have the law overturned on constitutional grounds, but a series of Supreme Court rulings upheld it.

These laws not only flexed the regulatory muscle of the U.S. government, they also marked a period in American history in which drug control policy was executed through taxation. Criminalization of drug use did not come via prohibition of possession, distribution, or production. Instead, during this period criminal charges were pinned on those skirting tax requirements. This system reflects a type of government power still used today—the use of tax penalties or incentives to stimulate preferred behaviors. Tax policy can be an effective behavioral incentive, not requiring but spurring individuals to make specific choices that the government believes creates social benefits. People are allowed to purchase cigarettes, but the federal government and state governments impose taxes in efforts both to generate revenue and to reduce use. Conversely, the government offers tax deductions for people who attend college, own a home, and make energy-efficient improvements to their dwellings.

In the case of drug policy, a taxation regime sought to raise revenue and incentivize certain behaviors among consumers and doctors—namely, they would no longer prescribe opium as a maintenance drug for addicts.[3] Much of the regulation of drugs during the early part of the twentieth century fell to the U.S. Department of Agriculture's (USDA's) Bureau of Chemistry, but as drug control policy expanded in scope, the administrative state regulatory structure expanded as well. In 1922 the Jones-Miller Act established the Narcotics Control Board and limited the importation of opium and cocaine into the United States except as authorized by the board (the secretaries of state, treasury, and commerce). It expanded criminal penalties for illegal importation and put restrictions on the ability to export narcotic drugs.

At this time, opium was seen as a worldwide problem, and the Jones-Miller Act was passed to comply with the recently ratified treaty emerging from the International Opium Convention, signed in 1912. Fears about addiction to opium were legitimate, but opium also elicited xenophobic fears about Asian immigrants and cultures. With this act, U.S. drug control policy began to shift away from an explicit taxation regime, as the early elements of drug prohibition were introduced.

PLANTING THE SEEDS OF MARIJUANA PROHIBITION   By the late 1920s the existing drug regulation apparatus needed reform. In 1927, Congress reorganized the Bureau of Chemistry, the government's most authoritative drug regulator, and renamed it the Food, Drug, and Insecticide Administration. This agency served as a new regulatory body and operated alongside its law enforcement peer, the Narcotics Commission, housed in the Bureau of Prohibition. In 1930 the name of the new regulatory body was shortened to the Food and Drug Administration (FDA).

The year 1930 brought other, more dramatic administrative changes. Congress passed H.R. 11143, the Porter Narcotic Bill, named after its sponsor, Congressman Stephen G. Porter (R-Pa.).[4] This law closed the Narcotics Control Board and transferred all the powers of the Narcotics Commission from the Bureau of Prohibition to the new Bureau of Narcotics within the Treasury Department. It gave the bureau broad law enforcement jurisdiction over the control of narcotic drugs in the United States. That administrative change, and the personnel choices that followed, were significant and had lasting effects.

On the recommendation of Congressman Porter, President Herbert Hoover selected as the first commissioner of the newly established Bureau of Narcotics Harry J. Anslinger, a veteran of the Bureau of Prohibition, whose early career had focused primarily on enforcing laws banning alcohol under Prohibition.[5] The new appointment allowed Anslinger to transfer the criminalization of alcohol use to other substances.

Anslinger's tenure began in late summer 1930 and lasted into the Kennedy administration. He may not have been America's first drug warrior, but he was certainly among its most passionate, and the one who had the greatest impact on drug policy in the twentieth century. He would play a central role in managing drug policy in the United States, ensuring that the power of the state and the specter of prohibition were ever expanding.

Commissioner Anslinger's drug portfolio was broad, but he had a special interest in marijuana. His activities in service of his anti-marijuana cause came to include touring the country and giving speeches to police groups, civic organizations, and others detailing the reasons marijuana was anathema. Anslinger engaged many of the same types of groups—women, police, local civic organizations—that composed the temperance movement, despite America's failed experience with alcohol prohibition. In many ways the two movements functioned similarly. Like alcohol, marijuana was painted as a scourge on society, ruining the moral fabric of America, breaking up families, and decreasing Americans' capacity for gainful employment.

Anslinger used or manipulated data to come up with creative statistics and compelling anecdotes. Anslinger's publicly cited "statistics" likely were "generalized from arrest rates or, perhaps, simply guessed."[6] If his use of statistics was creative, his marijuana narrative was over the top. In one 1937 essay Anslinger wrote, "No one knows, when he places a marijuana cigarette to his lips, whether he will become a philosopher, a joyous reveler in a musical heaven, a mad insensate, a calm philosopher, or a murderer."[7] The essay is a stream of vignettes in which young people who use marijuana rob, rape, and murder strangers, police officers, even members of their own families.

Racism became commonplace in Anslinger's discussion of marijuana, including coded language such as "The cigarettes may have been sold by a hot tamale vendor" or "Marijuana found a ready welcome . . . in a closely congested section of New York."[8] Anslinger could also be more explicit in his insinuations: "Marijuana was introduced into the United States from Mexico, and swept across America with incredible speed."[9]

This personal crusade combining scare tactics and racial overtones was quite effective at both the state and federal levels. Early in his tenure, Anslinger strongly supported passage of the Uniform State Narcotic Act of 1932 (its language had been drafted by the National Conference of Commissioners on Uniform State Laws), which pushed states both to unify their narcotics laws and to include cannabis under the "narcotic" designation. The act prescribed criminal punishments for those violating the laws at the state level.

Anslinger also was able to motivate Congress to act. In 1937, Congress passed the Marihuana Tax Act (using the then-current spelling). It was the first time the federal government used the word in any formal context. This law required anyone who "imports, manufactures, produces, compounds, sells, deals in, dispenses, prescribes, administers, or gives away marihuana" to register with the government and purchase a tax stamp from the Department of Treasury. Failure to do so resulted in sometimes draconian fines and terms of imprisonment. The Marihuana Tax Act of 1937 was an early U.S. government effort to criminalize all behavior involved in marijuana production. It would be just the beginning.

Prior to and during Anslinger's reign atop of the Bureau of Narcotics, America's approach to marijuana changed dramatically. In the years after the Mexican-American

War (1846–48), as hundreds of thousands of Mexican immigrants streamed across the border, racial tensions heated up. As Americans sought a pretext to vilify this new immigrant community, they found an ideal culprit in marijuana, a more common crop south of the border and a substance used for a variety of purposes in Mexican culture at the time. Starting early in the twentieth century, fear and anti-immigrant sentiment prompted state-level bans on cannabis; this movement accelerated during Anslinger's tenure and was harmonized after passage of the Uniform State Narcotic Act in 1932. While the federal government sought to tax and regulate drugs, states began outlawing them, particularly marijuana.

Although many Americans bought into Anslinger's propaganda about the evils and dangers of marijuana, it failed to convince everyone. The passage of the Marijuana Tax Act of 1937 and subsequent regulatory legislation like the Food, Drug, and Cosmetic Act of 1938 also met with some resistance, and some medical professionals, public officials, and politicians pushed back.[10] The most notable, highest-profile challenge to Anslinger came from Fiorello La Guardia, the mayor of New York City, who formed the La Guardia Committee to study the effects of marijuana in the United States and examine Anslinger's claims. In 1944 the committee published the La Guardia Report, and compared to the information pouring out of the Bureau of Narcotics, the information this report contained was stunning. It declared that marijuana was not addictive, was not motivating major crimes, and was not common among children. Ultimately, the report declared—a clear rebuke of Anslinger—"The publicity concerning the catastrophic effects of marihuana smoking in New York City is unfounded."[11]

Anslinger was not pleased; the backlash was severe. As Martin Lee profiles in *Smoke Signals: A Social History of Marijuana—Medical, Recreational and Scientific*, Anslinger's response was multifaceted. Anslinger "called the La Guardia Report a 'government printed invitation to youth and adults—above all teenagers—to go ahead and smoke all the reefers they feel like.'" Anslinger also lobbied the American Medical Association and the American Pharmaceutical Association to publicly criticize the report, effectively neutering its impact.[12] This was just one battle among many in the policy discussion around marijuana specifically and drugs more generally.

Some in the medical community sought to deal with marijuana users through treatment programs. In fact, the Porter Act explicitly directed the surgeon general to create and administer treatment facilities for drug addicts. Others still felt that the most effective drug policy was a revenue-based regulatory system. For Anslinger, that was not enough—criminalization was the only option. Ultimately, criminalization won the day. To achieve this end, Anslinger constantly conveyed to Americans and, more important, to Congress the notion that marijuana use was widespread and growing and that the most effective strategy to deal with it was punishment. He scored victories before Congress in 1951 with the passage of the Boggs Act and in 1956 with the Narcotics Control Act. The Boggs Act set mandatory minimum prison sentences for drug law violators. The Narcotics Control Act increased those penalties. By the late 1950s, drugs, and in particular marijuana, were legal but very difficult to procure legally (through a doctor), and procuring pot illegally resulted in serious punishment. The criminalization of drugs in the United States was in force and Harry Anslinger was in command, continuing to push for stricter laws and peddling scare stories and statistics to advance his cause.

THREE MARIJUANA AS AN ENEMY, FOREIGN AND DOMESTIC

THE 1960S BROUGHT DRAMATIC social change in the United States, and in many ways, marijuana was at the center of it. The decade was ushered in by beatniks and out by hippies, two counterculture movements that pushed back against social and cultural norms and controversial government policies. Hippies protested what they considered an unjust government, an unjust war, an unjust society. This movement was about freedom, civil rights, peace, and whatever else young people felt needed to be changed.

As the American government fought a foreign militia in Southeast Asia, the government and establishment found themselves battling a perceived scourge domestically. This enemy was not clad in fatigues, blending into the jungle thicket. Instead, it donned long hair, tie-dyed shirts, and handmade signs. It inhabited bohemian neighborhoods of big cities and college campuses across the nation. The movement responded not to the commands of a sergeant but to the cacophony of a new type of music and the chants of protest leaders using bullhorns.

The youth movement transformed American thinking for decades to come and made older generations nervous. Worried about their boys overseas, Americans also worried about the fabric of their society at home. Those tensions were linked. Youths associated with the counterculture were painted as less valuable than youths drafted into war. That conflict intensified feelings on both sides, driving the protests to grow louder and the government's response to be stronger.

The counterculture movement generated not only concern among parents, campus leaders, and local law enforcement but also reactions from the FBI, Congress, and the president of the United States. As young people burned draft cards and bras, listened to new kinds of music, relaxed their attitudes about sex and sexuality, and dressed differently from their parents, the one area that seemed to crystallize all the negatives of the counterculture was drugs—specifically, marijuana.

Marijuana played an outsized role in the music scene and other creative media, and its use began to expand among a younger generation. The decade in which marijuana may have most notably transformed elements of society also helped transform the perspective of government and, ultimately, the government's response. The counterculture struck fear into the establishment elements of society and motivated government to strike back. The response was increased criminalization of drugs, including marijuana, in an effort to roll back the countercultural revolution and bring American society back to an earlier era.

The groundwork for these efforts was laid even before the 1960s arrived. In November 1954, President Dwight D. Eisenhower appointed the Interdepartmental Committee on Narcotics, its membership drawn from all of his cabinet departments. The committee's brief was "to make a comprehensive up to date survey on the extent of narcotic addiction, in order to define more clearly the scope of the problems and to promote effective co-operation among federal states and local agencies. Determination of what the states and local agencies had accomplished and what they were equipped to do in the field of law enforcement and in the rehabilitation of the victims was to be included."[1] The committee delivered its report to President Eisenhower on February 1, 1956. The report relied heavily on statistics from the Bureau of Narcotics and its focus was exclusively on the harms that drugs wrought on society and individuals. Its fourteen recommendations foreshadowed the following thirty years of drug policy in the United States.

The first recommendation of the Eisenhower report (as I shall refer to it in this book) was to "encourage continuing studies of the narcotics problem within the states and municipalities," once again focusing exclusively on harm and how to reduce such harm. This would become a major tenet of drug policy in the latter half of the twentieth century. The ninth recommendation laid out what would become the nation's drug education programs, detailing how youth should be taught about the dangers and ills of drugs. The tenth recommendation focused on crime and offered insight into what would become the harsh government attitudes toward drug use and its punishment, stating:

> The Committee arrived at the conclusion that there was a need for a continuation of the policy of punishment of a severe character as a deterrent to narcotic law violations. It therefore recommended an increase of maximum sentences for first as well as subsequent offences. With respect to mandatory minimum features of such penalties, and prohibition of suspended sentences or probation, the Committee fully recognized objections in principle. It felt, however, that, in order to define the gravity of this class of crime and the assured penalty to follow, these features of the law must be regarded as essential elements of the desired deterrents.[2]

The final recommendation in the Eisenhower report drew attention to marijuana, linking narcotic drug abuse with its use and recommending further research. The committee told the president that drug use must be dealt with through harsh criminalization, regardless of mitigating factors. That message would come to be adopted through a variety of pieces of legislation (discussed later).

The main thrust of the Eisenhower report was to create a robust apparatus to investigate not *whether* drugs were harmful, but the depths of that harm for society, and to establish an administrative state that would punish violators with harsh sentences. The Eisenhower report reflected the U.S. government's drive to expand state power and criminalize drug use and abuse, domestically and internationally. As the Eisenhower report was being drafted, the United Nations was actively working on a convention to deal with drug use, abuse, manufacture, trade, and commerce worldwide.[3] The Single Convention on Narcotic Drugs, published in 1961, was the international community's first broad-based, prohibition-centered effort to control the international trade in drugs.[4] The stated goal of the convention was to deal with drug abuse and addiction throughout the world. It created the International Narcotics Control Board and developed a list of "schedules" to classify drugs according to relative levels of danger and likelihood of creating an addiction.

Schedule I drugs were the most addictive, hence the most tightly controlled, and the convention placed marijuana in this group. Indeed, the final recommendation in the report drew attention to marijuana, linking narcotic drug abuse with its use and recommending further research. Paragraph 1 of the convention's article 28, "Control of Cannabis," requires cannabis to be controlled the same as opium and charges member nations to enact laws to stop addiction.[5] Although the convention states that member nations can allow medical and scientific uses for Schedule I drugs, such as cannabis, restrictions on its manufacture and distribution are substantial. In many ways, the convention sought to outlaw cannabis, and at a minimum, gave member states the license and motivation to do so.

As the United States mulled over the decision whether to endorse the convention or not, an ongoing debate on drug policy was taking place in the United States, even into the next administration, that of President John F. Kennedy. On January 15, 1963, President Kennedy signed Executive Order 11076, "Establishing the President's

Advisory Commission on Narcotic and Drug Abuse." The Advisory Commission took a deep dive into the chemical and physiological impacts of individual drugs, their relationship with addiction, and the public policies that could achieve intended outcomes. The report read something like the La Guardia Report from two decades before. The Advisory Commission noted that the government needed to invest much more in research into questions about drugs, medical uses, and addiction. It stated that drugs that are often grouped together legally are very different in terms of addiction risk and effects on the body. The report also pushed back directly on the report prepared for President Eisenhower, arguing that for low-level drug offenses, the social and financial costs of hypercriminalization were too high. The report even went so far as to say that mandatory minimum sentences should be reconsidered. In a period in which the U.S. government and UN seemed to be trying to stoke fear about drugs and impose greater control and criminalization of their use, the Advisory Commission report served as the voice of moderation. Its recommendations, however, would not come to fruition, as the report was delivered to the president just days before his final trip to Dallas.

Kennedy's successor, Lyndon Johnson, was conflicted on drug policy. He was president during some of the most explosive days of the counterculture revolution, and he was its prime target. Antiwar and other protests were occurring across the country, and in front of the White House. The president saw drug use as part of these movements. He also saw soldiers returning from Southeast Asia addicted to a variety of drugs—an additional problem layered atop the Vietnam quagmire.

At the same time, the Johnson administration offered some rays of hope for those seeking a change in course in America's drug policy. Harry Anslinger had retired as head of the Bureau of Narcotics in 1962, and completed a short stint on the UN's narcotics board until 1964, after which time the U.S. government no longer sought Anslinger's counsel on drug policy. The Advisory Commission report recommended reforming the nation's drug policy bureaucracy—a direct challenge to the Bureau of Narcotics. This reform proposal would move part of the drug policy responsibility from the exclusive control of law enforcement agencies in Justice and Treasury to the Department of Health, Education, and Welfare (HEW).[6]

That move was formalized by the passage of the Drug Abuse Control Amendments of 1965, which expanded the powers of the secretary of HEW to make determinations about the classifications of drugs.[7] In early 1966 HEW established the Bureau of Drug Abuse Control to administer this expanded authority, which was housed in the Food and Drug Administration.[8]

President Johnson saw drug use and its connection to crime as a serious problem for the nation, but also as a public health crisis, often distinguishing between users and dealers. In his 1966 Special Message to Congress on Crime and Law Enforcement, Johnson noted a recent rise in the seizure of drugs, including marijuana. However, in a statement, bold for its time from an American president, he stated, "Our continued insistence on treating drug addicts, once apprehended, as criminals, is neither humane nor effective. It has neither curtailed addiction nor prevented crime." A comprehensive new drug treatment plan, based on this sentiment, would have been seismic in nature, pushing back against the tsunami of laws and policies seeking to criminalize drug use. However, given the president's standing and the rapidly deteriorating situation in Vietnam, Johnson was unable to reform drug laws before withdrawing from reelection. He was succeeded by Richard Nixon. Any hope of reforming America's drug laws—treating users as patients rather than prisoners, and distinguishing marijuana from highly habit-forming narcotics—were all dashed by the 1968 election. If Harry Anslinger was a foot soldier in the fight against drugs, Richard Nixon was America's first drug warrior.

FOUR RICHARD NIXON FIRES THE OPENING SHOTS IN THE WAR ON DRUGS

WHILE LYNDON JOHNSON at times acknowledged treating drug use and addiction as a public health problem, Richard Nixon believed drugs to be a criminal element and a scourge on society—their use to be punished, their existence to be stamped out.

President Nixon was a man riddled with fear and paranoia and one who often vented his frustration toward "otherness"—on blacks, Jews, foreigners, women, Democrats, Congress, even his own staff, and whomever else he perceived as a threat. Drugs and drug users were one such threat, as was the counterculture movement, which Nixon despised. Nixon inherited from Johnson a war and a "drug-fueled" hippie movement, and he sought to end both. Within those efforts is an irony. The president who ultimately extracted the United States from one of its most protracted wars would launch the nation on its longest, most enduring conflict: the War on Drugs.

Richard Nixon often framed the War on Drugs as a policy-driven effort to root drug abuse out of American society. The reality was much more complex. No doubt Nixon saw drugs as a problem and a threat. His own battles with alcoholism perhaps offered him familiarity with the ills of substance abuse. However, the War on Drugs also fit into Nixon's broader political strategy. Nixon's well-known Southern Strategy sought to vilify out-groups in society, particularly racial minorities and members of the counterculture. It capitalized on white Americans' fears of a changing society and sought to shift blame for these changes onto the integration of schools, crime, drug use, urban unrest, and the quest for civil rights. In fact, Nixon's White House counsel, John Ehrlichman, has been quoted as explicitly stating that Nixon's drug policies were racially motivated.[1]

These political efforts were a pushback against Johnson administration policies and the social upheaval of the 1960s. Drug use both created fears and gave Nixon fuel to further stoke those fears. It also intertwined with long-term government rhetoric that drug use, especially marijuana use, had been introduced to the United States by Asian and Mexican immigrants and that the use was predominantly among black populations. That targeting of use and scapegoating allowed Nixon to paint an effective "us versus them" scenario that could be extended to electoral arenas, particularly by peddling the worry that *those* groups could infect innocents with such drugs. The War on Drugs was as much about getting Richard Nixon reelected in 1972 as it was about eliminating drugs from American society. Of course, no armistice was signed at the start of Nixon's second term, nor as he exited the presidency in disgrace two and a half years later.

WAR PLANNING AND STRATEGY Even before President Nixon officially declared a war on drugs, his drug policy shifted in dramatic ways, in part rhetorical and in part statutory. In his first year in office, Nixon discussed combatting drug use on numerous occasions—in speeches, messages to Congress, and executive actions. On July 14, 1969, Nixon told Congress that drug abuse was "a serious national threat to the personal health and safety of millions of Americans."[2] With the commonplace rhetoric of drug policy, he went on to put the consequences into a horrifying yet digestible context for Congress and the public: "Street robberies, prostitution, even enticing of others into addiction to drugs—an addict will reduce himself to any offense, any degradation in order to acquire the drugs he craves."[3] Nixon's address included a ten-point plan, focused largely on empowering law enforcement and expanding punishment. Only one plank of the plan addressed rehabilitation of addicts, but with the explicit caveat that "this sickness cannot excuse the crimes they commit."[4]

Nixon's actions went beyond rhetoric. The first shot in what would become Nixon's new War on Drugs began in response to a court case. On May 19, 1969—less than four months into the Nixon presidency—the United States Supreme Court handed down a decision in *Leary v. United States*.[5] The case was significant for the future of drug policy and likely had a substantial effect on what would become Nixonian activism on the issue. Timothy Leary, a Harvard professor, was arrested at the U.S.-Mexico border for possessing marijuana, and was charged with violating the Marijuana Tax Act. He sued, claiming that the law violated his Fifth Amendment right against self-incrimination, as it required him to admit possessing an illegal substance because he had an obligation to pay taxes on it under the act. Ultimately the Court agreed and ruled the Marijuana Tax Act of 1937—one of the country's most significant pieces of marijuana legislation—unconstitutional.

Just a few months later, in September 1969, Nixon and John Ingersoll, the head of the new Bureau of Narcotics and Dangerous Drugs (the successor to the Bureau of Narcotics), authorized Operation Intercept, a multiday effort to shutter the U.S.-Mexico border to search vehicles for illegal drugs. The expensive operation yielded relatively little in terms of seizures of contraband, led to an aggressive counteroperation by the Mexican government, and was widely considered a failure—except within the White House.[6] On October 23, 1969, President Nixon organized the Bipartisan Leadership Meeting on Narcotics and Dangerous Drugs, and after delivering opening remarks, he introduced Ingersoll and offered him an opportunity to heap praise upon Operation Intercept. Nixon explained, "Operation Intercept was very, very successful. While it was in effect, and even to this day, the flow of narcotics and marihuana from Mexico into this country was substantially curtailed. Marihuana is still in short supply in the United States, and in most places where it is available, at least the Mexican form, the prices have doubled and in some cases tripled."[7] Contemporary and historical accounts of Operation Intercept suggest that in making these comments Nixon was divorced from reality.[8]

ARMING GENERAL NIXON AND HIS CONSCRIPTS

Besides his rhetorical efforts to put the drug problem into his preferred context and his cheerleading for the administration's drug control efforts, the president also sought legislative paths toward expanded federal power to control drugs. In 1970 he took up the cause of bringing the United States into line with the United Nations Single Convention on Narcotic Drugs. Working with Congress, the president signed the Comprehensive Drug Abuse Prevention and Control Act of 1970, more commonly known as the Controlled Substances Act (CSA).[9]

This law formalized the drug scheduling construct prescribed in the Single Convention. Under CSA, there would be five drug schedules ranging from Schedule I to Schedule V. Schedule I would be reserved for what Congress and subsequently regulatory agencies would deem the most dangerous, most heavily regulated substances (conversely, Schedule V substances would receive the lowest level of control). Under Schedule I, substances were given a label that would become the trifecta of prohibition. Under CSA's section 202(b)(1), a Schedule I substance:

A) . . . has a high potential for abuse,
B) . . . has no currently accepted medical use in treatment in the United States, and
C) . . . there is a lack of accepted safety for use of the drug or other substance under medical supervision.

Rather than leaving the classifications of drugs up to the FDA or the scientific and medical communities post-passage, Congress sorted drugs into the five categories itself. It placed marijuana in Schedule I, along with opium, LSD, and methamphetamines. Notably, and because of widespread use and entrenched political interests, alcohol and tobacco did not fall under the jurisdiction of CSA. The lack of control occurred despite both substances being highly addicting and have no medical value. Both substances were left to be regulated under their own separate systems, despite significant overlap in characteristics with controlled substances.

The CSA dramatically expanded government power over and regulation of drugs. The law set up processes to deal with adding and removing substances as well as recategorizing a substance in a different schedule (rescheduling). It was the most comprehensive prohibition of substances in American history.

No one was more pleased with the passage of this law than President Richard Nixon. At a White House ceremony on October 27, 1970, he issued a signing statement on the Controlled Substances Act in which he did not mince words about what CSA would mean for drug abuse:

> We can deal with it. We have the laws now. We are going to go out and enforce those laws. But in order for those laws to mean anything they must have public support. . . . And therefore, I hope that at the time the Federal Government is moving, as we are moving very strongly in this field, that the whole Nation will join with us in a program to stop the rise in the use of

drugs and thereby help to stop the rise in crime; and also save the lives of hundreds of thousands of our young people who otherwise would become hooked on drugs and be physically, mentally, and morally destroyed.[10]

In this signing statement, Richard Nixon accomplished multiple goals. He wanted the CSA to change America's drug policy in dramatic ways. First, he lauded the legislation, signaling the substantial White House support not just for its passage but for ensuring it would be applied. Second, he explicitly sought to sway public support in favor of what would come to be America's aggressive effort to control drugs in unprecedented ways. Third, he framed the discussion of drug abuse not as an isolated issue in big cities or among suspect groups of people but instead spoke of the widespread threat that drugs posed to all of America's youth and offered the CSA as an antidote to this threat and a savior of the children.

Ultimately, much of what Richard Nixon wanted would come to fruition. Public opinion would rally behind the effort to control drugs and drug abuse, and the CSA would dramatically change the nature of drug policy in the United States. This legislation has influenced public policy to this day.

A "DECLARATION" OF WAR ON DRUGS   The CSA gave President Nixon the statutory means to begin a broad-based, long-term effort to rid the nation of drugs, drug abuse, and drug users through regulation, criminalization, and (a low priority) treatment. The president was on a mission.

This mission would not be isolated or concentrated. It would not be a surgical strike or a special ops mission. It would be a war.

Under Article I Section 8 of the United States Constitution, Congress has the power to declare war. Of course, it is hard to declare war on a plant or a cigarette or a bottle of pills or a group of users within the borders of the United States. Yet to President Nixon and many in Congress, drugs such as marijuana were as dangerous as any foreign enemy, putting at risk the lives and well-being of millions of Americans.

Nixon declared his War on Drugs on June 17, 1971, less than eight months after the passage of the Controlled Substances Act. On that day, President Nixon also announced the appointment of Jerome Jaffe as special consultant to the president for narcotics and dangerous drugs and issued Executive Order No. 11599, which established the Special Action Office for Drug Abuse Prevention, created the new position of director to lead the office, and outlined the mission and jurisdiction of the office.

Even though the declaration of war was informal, the way the War on Drugs was waged—the funding, organization, planning, strategy, and missions—looked at times like the waging of war in Vietnam, Korea, and other foreign conflicts. And Nixon used language to match. His words dripped with the language of war—as if the Pentagon had punched up these messages to Americans. In his remarks at a White House Press briefing in June 1971, Nixon stated,

> America's public enemy number one in the United States is drug abuse. In order to fight and defeat this enemy, it is necessary to wage a new, all-out offensive.

I have asked the Congress to provide the legislative authority and the funds to fuel this kind of an offensive. . . . If we are going to have a successful offensive, we need more money. . . . Finally, in order for this program to be effective, it is necessary that it be conducted on a basis in which the American people all join in it.[11]

This phrase "drug abuse" could have been replaced with "Nazis" and the message easily confused with a World War II–era statement sent from the FDR White House. It combined a focus on an enemy, a request for money—the equivalent of an emergency war supplemental—and a rallying of Americans to a cause reminiscent of exhortations to purchase war bonds and cultivate victory gardens.

In his "Special Message to Congress on Drug Abuse Prevention and Control," Nixon claimed that the new Controlled Substances Act was insufficient to the broader task and made an emotional appeal to rally Congress to approve his war funds:

Narcotics addiction is a problem which afflicts both the body and the soul of America. It is a problem which baffles many Americans. In our history we have faced great difficulties again and again, wars and depressions and divisions among our people have tested our will as a people—and we have prevailed. We have fought together in war, we have worked together in hard times, and we have reached out to each other in division—to close the gaps between our people and keep America whole. The threat of narcotics among our people is one which properly frightens many Americans. It comes quietly into homes and destroys children, it moves into neighborhoods and breaks the fiber of community which makes neighbors. . . . The final issue is not whether we will conquer drug abuse, but how soon. Part of this answer lies with the Congress now and the speed with which it moves to support the struggle against drug abuse.[12]

President Nixon identified the enemy, laid out a plan of attack, and asked for the support to accomplish the task, but also built in a strategic effort the help guarantee his success. He immediately distinguished himself as a leader, ready to fight an insidious enemy, and shifted responsibility for fighting this enemy (and prospective blame in the case of failure) to Congress.

Ultimately, Richard Nixon's efforts were resoundingly successful. Less than a year after Nixon declared his War on Drugs, Congress approved his war supplemental. On March 16, 1972, the House and Senate approved the Drug Abuse Office and Treatment Act of 1972. The House vote was 366–0; the Senate's, 92–0.[13] The appropriations contained in this legislation gave Nixon the additional funding he needed to prosecute the war as he saw fit. And so the United States entered an unprecedented War on Drugs—one that historically was a series of smaller-scale battles. President Nixon ramped up the campaign and ultimately handed the war off to his successors, who as commanders-in-chief would strategize and prosecute this war in their own ways.

FIVE PROSECUTING THE WAR ON DRUGS

ONE OF THE EARLY battles Nixon faced grew out of the Controlled Substances Act itself, Section 601, which established the National Commission on Marihuana and Drug Abuse. Nixon, who appointed nine of the commission's thirteen members, likely saw the commission as an opportunity to produce propaganda in support of the War on Drugs—the commission was tasked with producing a report on drug use.[1] Many members of Congress praised the creation of the commission, while several other members raised questions about marijuana: its effects, its inclusion in the Controlled Substances Act, and specifically in Schedule I. Representative Gilbert Gude (R-Md.) was one of these, stating on the House floor on September 24, 1970:

> I am particularly pleased by the section establishing the Commission on Marihuana and Drug Abuse.

I sponsored legislation to establish a Marijuana Commission which was approved by the Judiciary Committee. This section owes much to the thought and effort of the Gentleman from New York [Democratic Congressman Ed Koch]. I hope the Commission can clear up some of the confusion and conflicting reports that have made it so difficult to formulate a sound policy on marihuana.[2]

Whereas Gude raised concerns and questions about the commission, Nixon had clear opinions about marijuana and obvious expectations about the value of the work of the well-funded ($1 million) commission.[3]

President Nixon selected Raymond Shafer—a former Pennsylvania governor, a Republican, and an old friend—as chairman of the commission. Commission members and staff began working in spring of 1971, and the final report, "Marihuana: A Signal of Misunderstanding," was delivered to President Nixon and Congress in March 1972. Nixon expected it to provide him with ammo in the drug war, but he didn't get what he wanted. Like the La Guardia Report before it, the Shafer Commission's report infuriated those in government who were committed to marijuana prohibition, chief among them the president of the United States.

The report explicitly opposed the legalization of recreational marijuana, stating, "Society should not approve or encourage the recreational use of any drug, in public or private. Any semblance of encouragement enhances the possibility of abuse and removes, from a psychological standpoint, an effective support of individual restraint."[4] However, the report forcefully challenged the historical, scientific, legal, and sociological underpinnings of the prohibition of marijuana. It challenged earlier policy choices: Were they the result of sound analysis or of historical and cultural biases built on false assumptions? It questioned the legitimacy of reports connecting the use of marijuana with increases in criminal activity.

The report also explored the societal and financial costs of criminalizing the possession and use of marijuana. In the face of a prohibition-centered War on Drugs, the Shafer report was damning, stating, "The Commission is of the unanimous opinion that marihuana use is not such a grave problem that individuals who smoke marihuana, and possess it for that purpose, should be subject to criminal procedures."

"Marihuana: A Signal of Misunderstanding" was transmitted to Congress and the president just days after the passage of the Drug Abuse Office and Treatment Act, which funded an expansion of the War on Drugs. Nixon expressed his concerns over the report unambiguously in advance of its publication. During an Oval Office meeting with Chairman Shafer on March 22, 1972, Nixon made his interests clear and sought to steer Shafer away from the type of report Nixon now expected:

> You're enough of a pro to know that for you to come out with something that would run counter to what the Congress feels and what the country feels and what we're planning to do, would make your Commission just look bad as hell. And I think in, I think that, and on the other hand, you could probably render a great service, that doesn't mean we're going to tell you what it's going to be, but we're going into this too.[5]

Nixon was unable to prevail upon his friend, and the report ended up reflecting some of Nixon's greatest fears. During a news conference a few days after the report's release, the president was asked about his reaction to it. His public statement on the report was brief, dismissive, and clear:

I met with Mr. Shafer. I have read the report. It is a report which deserves consideration and it will receive it. However, as to one aspect of the report, I am in disagreement. I was before I read it, and reading it did not change my mind. I oppose the legalization of marihuana and that includes its sale, its possession, and its use. I do not believe that you can have effective criminal justice based on a philosophy that something is half legal and half illegal. That is my position, despite what the Commission has recommended.[6]

The report's release was timed badly for the president: Congress was debating appropriations for his Drug War efforts, and 1972 was an election year. Ultimately, though, Nixon was able to sideline the report, avoid fallout, and continue with his War on Drugs. Having largely won the battle against Ray Shafer, Nixon pushed forward with his reelection campaign. His strategy was to use drugs as a wedge issue to stoke fear in voters and drive them to his cause, and he mentioned drugs in no fewer than twenty-four official statements between September 1 and Election Day. On October 28, 1972, less than two weeks before the election, Nixon held a campaign rally in Cleveland, Ohio, and claimed credit for dramatic reductions in drug use in the United States, attributing those successes to his administration's efforts. He closed his speech talking about what he wanted to do in the next four years, and with the typical din of dog-whistle politics told the audience, "By winning the war on crime and drugs, we can restore the social climate of order and justice which will assure our society of the freedom it must have to build and grow."[7]

Eleven days later, Richard Nixon was reelected, winning more votes than any other president up to that point in history (over 47 million), carrying forty-nine states and earning 520 electoral votes. In his second term, Nixon did not change the direction of his drug policy, nor mute its aggression. He devoted his first State of the Union Address in his second term exclusively to drug abuse prevention, closing the speech by singling out marijuana and powerfully opposing its legalization.[8] Later that month, on March 28, 1973, Nixon took one of his last significant actions in the War on Drugs, when he submitted to Congress a request to allow the "Reorganization Plan 2 of 1973" to go into effect. Congress acceded and on July 1, the Drug Enforcement Administration was established in the Department of Justice. This change in the U.S. government's drug policy bureaucracy was the most significant in American history, both up to that time and since. The new agency would "absorb the associated manpower and budgets" of essentially all of the drug enforcement programs scattered throughout government departments and agencies: the Bureau of Narcotics and Dangerous Drugs, the portion of the Bureau of Customs portfolio "pertaining to drug investigations and intelligence," the Office for Drug Abuse Law Enforcement, and the Office of National Narcotics Intelligence.[9]

The new agency's jurisdiction, mission, manpower, and funding were substantial to begin with and would grow dramatically over time. In 1974 the DEA had 4,075 employees and a budget of $116 million ($557 million in 2014 dollars). By 1985 it had 4,936 employees and a budget of $362 million ($796 million in 2014 dollars). In 2014 it had 11,055 employees and a budget of $2.882 billion.[10] The DEA would engage not only in domestic drug enforcement but also would act internationally, working closely with the CIA and other agencies to extend the War on Drugs beyond the U.S. borders, particularly into Latin America.

Many of Richard Nixon's actions—rhetorical, statutory, and organizational—had and continue to have lasting effects on American drug policy. In addition to assisting law enforcement in administering drug policy centered nearly exclusively on criminalization, the DEA was used by Nixon's successors in new ways. Future presidents would rely heavily on the DEA to boost their "tough on crime, tough on drugs" bona fides. Presidents and Congress protected the administrative apparatus that empowered and enforced drug laws in the United States. The agency's annual budget shrank just once between 1974 and 2014.[11]

Nixon resigned in August 1974, but the War on Drugs raged on. President Gerald Ford largely carried on the work by engaging Latin American partners like Mexico and Colombia in an effort to interrupt the supply of illegal drugs, especially marijuana, from entering the country. Despite those efforts, President Ford admitted, American policy in this area was failing. In a message to Congress in 1976, he wrote, "By 1975, it was clear that drug use was increasing, that the gains of prior years were being lost."[12]

Yet Ford was a bit unpredictable on the issue of drugs. On the one hand he maintained the apparatus he inherited from President Nixon to root out drugs from society. He also offered some of the most aggressive rhetoric on the War on Drugs, perhaps even surpassing Nixon's in its militarism. In that same message to Congress, Ford wrote of prior drug control efforts:

Unfortunately, while we had won an important victory, we had not won the war on drugs. . . . Today, drug abuse constitutes a clear and present threat to the health and future of our Nation. The time has come to launch a new and more aggressive campaign to reverse the trend of increasing drug abuse in America. . . . Americans have always stood united and strong against all enemies. Drug abuse is an enemy we can control but there must be a personal and a national dedication and commitment to the goal.

One could imagine Ford singing Irving Berlin or Glenn Miller in his head as he, during a period of relative international peace, fancied himself a wartime president at home. Rather than mobilizing generals at the Pentagon, he coordinated efforts between the DEA and two newly established cabinet committees intended to deal with the "enemy."

On the other hand, aspects of Gerald Ford's drug control efforts were more moderate than Nixon's. He put a tremendous emphasis on treatment and prevention. In speeches and statements he eloquently conveyed that drug use and abuse was a public health issue rather than a public safety issue. In those contexts, he slung off the guise of Generalissimo Ford and became Gerald Ford, grandfather. He often referred to drug addicts as victims, subject to the criminal harms of traffickers (a group he showed a particular aggression toward), and as individuals in need of help. He showed compassion and what sounded like sympathy—but was likely empathy. In an October 1975 statement, Ford pulled back the curtain a bit, noting, "Drug abuse is a problem of deep personal concern to me."[13] It would come to light just a few years later that his wife, First Lady Betty Ford, had battled substance abuse for years and had sought help only after leaving the White House.

Given these circumstances one can understand that President Ford was torn. A tough-on-crime and tough-on-drugs stand had been a strategic electoral tool for his predecessor, and Ford would face the voters just twenty-seven months after assuming the presidency. At the same time, in his own family he saw drug addiction firsthand and recognized that treatment, rather than criminalization, was a more reasonable and humane approach to dealing with it. So Gerald Ford was a somewhat confusing combination of drug warrior and treatment advocate—probably not unlike many Americans at the time, quietly dealing with drug abuse under their own roofs.

In 1976 Ford lost to Jimmy Carter, a president who was as close to being a reformer as any president in American history. Yet Carter, too, was pulled in different directions by competing ideological forces, showing tendencies toward both supporting more government control and in other contexts tending toward libertarianism—reducing the presence of government in Americans' lives. The latter seemed to guide his approach to drug policy.

Carter despised drug trafficking and international narco-operations and spoke openly of seeking to suppress both. He sought additional law enforcement muscle to combat trafficking, and supported increasing the eligible levels of asset forfeiture and enhanced sentences for major traffickers. He also sought broader international cooperation to stem what he saw as the drug trade, not as an open military conflict, but actually as a trade—an economic operation. He recognized that factors of supply, demand, and pricing could have an impact on the flow of drugs across the border and sought to police accordingly. At the same time he did little to change the institutional apparatus of the drug war that his predecessors had constructed.

Instead, Carter's reformist tendencies were expressed in the staff he selected and the policies he supported. One of Carter's first opportunities to influence drug policy came with his choice to head the newly established Office of Drug Abuse Policy.[14] To head the office Carter selected a friend from Georgia, Dr. Peter Bourne, a known drug treatment specialist and reformer. In a March 1977 swearing-in ceremony Carter welcomed him warmly, saying that Bourne is "among my closest friends in the world . . . who helped me in Georgia to set up one of the finest drug treatment programs in the nation. . . . He's recognized as the foremost expert on alcoholism, drugs, their impact, and the way to control them properly." By White House standards, Bourne was a dramatic change agent.

Carter sought expanded federal research into drugs and drug policy and a more expansive federal drug treatment strategy and policy. Within that policy was a special plank for marijuana. Together, Carter and Bourne forged a proposal to decriminalize marijuana in the United States. Not only was Carter's proposal reformist in nature, his words were of a different type and tone for an American president. The proposal was progressive not just in its scope, but in the context of the presidency. Teddy Roosevelt and the eleven presidents who followed him had taken steps to enact more restrictive drug control policies. Carter's proposal was the first presidential effort to reverse the tide on an issue that had transformed some earlier commanders-in-chief into warmongering zealots.

In his 1977 "Drug Abuse Message to the Congress," Carter outlined his views on marijuana. In the drug reform community, one powerful line often stands out for containing some of the most reform-oriented language ever to come from a president on the subject of drugs: "Penalties against possession of a drug should not be more damaging to an individual than the use of the drug itself; and where they are, they should be changed. Nowhere is this more clear than in the laws against the possession of marijuana in private for personal use."[15] Carter followed up this statement of compassion, pushing back against the U.S. government's institutionalized system of criminalization, with his proposal: "I support legislation amending Federal law to eliminate all Federal criminal penalties for the possession of up to one ounce of marijuana. This decriminalization is not legalization. It means only that the Federal penalty for possession would be reduced and a person would receive a fine rather than a criminal penalty."

However, the reform community's near apostolic commitment to repeating this quotation overlooks some of the other, even more important parts of this message and what it reveals about the depth of reform that Carter had in mind. The message touched on five critical issues:

1. One aim of Carter's policy was to focus federal attention on more serious drugs that were statistically shown to "pose the greatest threat to health, and to our ability to reduce crime." Where previous presidents' efforts had focused on marijuana as anathema, Carter stated, "Since heroin, barbiturates and other sedative/hypnotic drugs account for 90 percent of the deaths from drug abuse, they should receive our principal emphasis."

2. Carter recognized that spreading drug policy jurisdiction across numerous federal agencies was inefficient and could easily lead to waste, fraud, and abuse. Carter sought to streamline the burgeoning bureaucracy.

3. Carter questioned the role of the federal government in drug enforcement, arguing that the federal government may have become too involved in policing drugs. The ever-expanding state power, spearheaded by Harry Anslinger and then ramped up by Richard Nixon, was likely too large and needed trimming. Carter was clear on this point: "I am directing my staff to recommend to me the appropriate Federal drug law enforcement. . . . For nearly a decade, federal support of state and local enforcement activity has steadily expanded. The

time is ripe to evaluate the results of this effort, to determine whether federal participation should be altered."

4. When it came to treatment, Carter wanted to look at drugs holistically, an idea that was otherwise nonexistent in the government rhetoric of the time. He was concerned with alcohol and tobacco, not just with marijuana, cocaine, and opiates. Carter's approach to treatment was that the goal of treatment should be "to help drug abusers return to productive lives." More than just helping addicts, treatment should truly rehabilitate them.

5. Carter acknowledged serious gaps in drug research in the United States. He didn't suggest that the policies of the United States government had caused those gaps, but he aimed to change the system for supporting research. He asked the Department of Health, Education, and Welfare to consider developing a federal clearinghouse that would coordinate research on all drugs to improve the scientific community's understanding of the issue.

The president's drug control agenda was aggressive and reform-oriented. Yet his reform vision never came to be—the proposals Carter laid out in his 1977 message to Congress would not be enacted. Dr. Bourne became embroiled in a political and personal scandal and ultimately resigned under a cloud. International affairs, fuel prices and crises, and inflation came to dominate the president's attention, taking focus away from drug reforms. Carter failed to win reelection in 1980, and the reform community's hope that drug policy change was on the horizon was soon dashed. In hindsight, Carter's efforts were the calm before the storm. His opponent in the 1980 election, Ronald Reagan, had no interest in drug policy reform. President Reagan instead recommitted to Nixon's War on Drugs, and expanded it.

SIX RONALD REAGAN OPENS NEW THEATERS IN THE WAR ON DRUGS

AFTER A PERIOD of moderation under the Carter administration, Ronald Reagan steered America back on course to a full-fledged War on Drugs. Reagan's drug war used additional federal spending for programs across the board that enhanced criminalization, pursued narco-traffickers, increased penalties for possession and use, and decreased court defenses; it also focused on education and expanded treatment.

In some ways, Reagan's approach looked quite a bit like Nixon's. Reagan saw Nixon's Southern Strategy and the racial issues that underpinned it as a path toward electoral success for him, too. Reagan dramatically expanded the fight against drugs beyond our borders, involving the United States in international drug-related conflicts and expanding programs such as drug eradication at the source, where the plants are grown and harvested. Under Reagan the DEA and other agencies worked at times with and at other times against some of Latin America's most feared dictators.

Early in his presidency, Reagan made a clear contrast between his administration's policy on drugs, specifically marijuana, and that of his predecessor. Reagan closed an October 1982 radio address with a tacit criticism of Carter: "The mood toward drugs is changing in this country, and the momentum is with us. We're making no excuses for drugs—hard, soft, or otherwise. Drugs are bad, and we're going after them. As I've said before, we've taken down the surrender flag and run up the battle flag. And we're going to win the war on drugs."[1] Explicit war rhetoric severed Reagan from Carter's drug reform. Reagan was ready for war and was in no way going to observe Carter's ceasefire.

That same radio address offered another glimpse into how Reagan's drug war would be different: the big departure had everything to do with whom he would enlist as his lieutenant—First Lady Nancy Reagan. That day Mrs. Reagan joined her husband in delivering the radio address on drug use in America.

Mrs. Reagan signaled her interest in making drug policy one of her priorities. She visited treatment centers and schools; she met with advocacy organizations and parents groups. She would ensure that the president did not ignore the drug problem in America. Nancy Reagan ultimately coined one of the most famous phrases in the history of the War on Drugs, "Just Say No," said in response to a question from a student at Longfellow Elementary in California in 1984. In all, she undertook 110 drug policy–related events in 1984.[2] The president ensured that the apparatus of government would combat drugs; Mrs. Reagan ensured that the public stayed engaged and aware of the battle, and knew that she was on the front-lines fighting for them.

Within the administration, the president took aggressive steps to ensure that government would fight drugs effectively. Southern Florida would serve as a focal point in this effort, as it served as a bridge for the flow of drugs into the United States from Latin America and other locales. A year into his presidency, Reagan tapped Vice President George H. W. Bush to lead the Federal Anti-crime Task Force for Southern Florida, an aggressive law enforcement operation to stop this supply route. Southern Florida would soon become a bridge of another kind—sending American antidrug operations into Latin America. During the twelve years of the Reagan and Bush administrations, American antidrug operations extended into Colombia, Mexico, Honduras, Panama, and other Latin American nations, to the extent that the War on Drugs came to look very much like a standard war against a foreign enemy.

Back in Washington, Reagan, like his predecessors, was committed to reorganizing and centralizing coordination of the war at the White House, specifically, in his new Drug Abuse Policy Office. Created by Executive Order No. 12368, the new entity, Reagan noted in a speech a few months later, was "responsible for overseeing all domestic and international drug functions. . . . There are nine departments and thirty-three agencies of Government that have some responsibility in the drug area, but until now, the activities of these agencies were not being coordinated. Each was fighting its own separate battle against drugs. Now, for the very first time, the Federal Government is waging a planned, concerted campaign."[3]

The new bureaucratic structure, redesigned to maximize the war effort, was bolstered by a series of legislative successes, of which the three most significant were the Comprehensive Crime Control Act of 1984, the Anti-Drug Abuse Act of 1986, and the Anti-Drug Abuse Act of 1988.[4] These laws differed in their emphasis, but one thing united them: they vastly enhanced criminal penalties for drug offenders, particularly dealers, traffickers, manufacturers, and repeat offenders. The 1986 law established mandatory minimums for a variety of additional drug crimes; several of those were enhanced under the 1988 law. Asset forfeiture was increased under both the 1986 and 1988 laws. Finally, the 1988 law gave authority to the president to create an office to increase policy coordination and educational efforts on drugs. Established in 1989 under President George H. W. Bush, the Office of National Drug Control Policy (ONDCP) replaced Reagan's Drug Abuse Policy Office. The director of the ONDCP came to be known as the drug czar.

Under Bush and his successors, the drug czar became a central powerful figure in the coordination and execution of U.S. drug policy. Part of the authorization for the office required the ONDCP to submit to Congress a national drug control strategy; in September 1989, led by its first director, Bill Bennett, the first such strategy was submitted, and on September 5, 1989, President Bush presented it in a prime-time address from the Oval Office. Using the tone of a father disciplining unruly teenagers, Bush laid out for Americans a four-point plan that constituted the next, more aggressive, chapter in the War on Drugs. He began by excoriating "everyone who uses drugs, everyone who sells drugs, and everyone who looks the other way," explaining that drugs are "murdering our children."[5]

The four-point plan was comprehensive, involving a variety of traditional avenues of combatting drugs, as well as some new ones, and foresaw substantial increases in federal funding to win the war. Bush asked Congress to "more than double assistance to State and local law enforcement . . . and enlarge our criminal justice system across the board." Like earlier campaigns, Bush's plan did not stop at the water's edge; he called for over a billion dollars for interdiction efforts in Latin America and openly asserted that he would use the U.S. military to fight the War on Drugs. The last two pegs in Bush's proposal involved spending billions of dollars on drug treatment and education.

In this speech Bush showed that when it came to waging the War on Drugs, he would be as tough as or even tougher than his predecessors. His newly created ONDCP and its drug czar would make sure of that.

TELLING THE CHILDREN The creation of the ONDCP was perhaps the element of the Anti-Drug Abuse Act that had the most lasting impact on American drug policy. However, the lengthy bill accomplished quite a bit in a variety of areas. The 1988 law vastly expanded funding for drug education. It amended numerous existing federal programs, redirecting funds toward drug policy. For example, the Child Nutrition Act of 1966 now included drug education alongside nutrition education for those receiving assistance. The nutrition program received an additional $10 million to study how to improve drug education efforts and to prepare and distribute education materials based on the study.

Drug education certainly did not begin with the Anti-Drug Abuse Act of 1988. One could trace drug education efforts back quite some time. The production in the late 1930s of propaganda films such as *Reefer Madness* (originally titled *Tell Your Children*) was intended to indoctrinate children and their parents as to the extreme danger of drugs, especially marijuana, and to motivate them to resist the temptation to use such substances.

Education was also an important consideration in more mainstream government documents. For example, the 1956 Eisenhower report recommended drug education. The approach was clear-eyed, stressing the importance of drug education while also recommending some caution. Recommendation nine in the report notes, "Special information concerning narcotic drugs in texts and curricula in schools [should be] carried out with extreme care, [as] such programmes might have the undesirable effect of attracting attention to and curiosity over experimentation with drugs." The recommendation also urged caution when "sponsoring motion picture, television, and radio treatment of the subject."[6]

Later presidents, including Richard Nixon, stressed education as a way to dissuade children from experimenting with drugs, but the efforts were basically to no avail, as usage rates among the young rose throughout much of the mid-twentieth century, especially in the 1960s. A more coordinated approach to drug education was developed in the 1980s. Thus, the Reagan era was transformational not only for the law enforcement and intelligence aspects of the War on Drugs but also for drug education.

In 1983, the Los Angeles Chief of Police, Daryl Gates, together with the Los Angeles Unified School District, founded the program Drug Abuse Resistance Education (D.A.R.E.) in response to the youth drug problems they saw in the jurisdiction. The program rapidly became a nationwide effort engaging federal, state, and local law enforcement and enlisting the help of local school districts to teach children about drugs. The following year, Nancy Reagan coined the catchphrase "Just Say No," a watershed moment that inadvertently launched a historic messaging campaign targeting America's youth. Nancy Reagan's catchphrase may have arisen by happenstance, but her commitment to antidrug policy had not. Prior to her years in the White House, while Ronald Reagan served as California's governor, she had a long track record of spearheading state-level efforts. Once in the White House, she was able to take that message national.

That movement connected with both parent and student groups as well as governments across the country to step up education efforts. In 1986, the Partnership for a Drug-Free America (now called Partnership for Drug-Free Kids) was founded as "an anti-drug advertising campaign . . . dedicated to reducing teen substance abuse and helping families impacted by addiction."[7] In 1987, this organization produced one of the most iconic antidrug public service advertisements ever—a short video featuring an egg (your brain), cracked and dropped into a hot cast-iron pan (drugs), and ending with a shot of the frying egg and the statement "This is your brain on drugs."[8]

All of these efforts were aided by the Anti-Drug Abuse Act of 1988, not least because of the creation of the ONDCP. The ONDCP coordinated many of the nation's drug education efforts; eventually the federal government ended up partnering with and helping fund the "Just Say No" campaign and D.A.R.E. program and working closely with the Partnership for a Drug-Free America to provide continuous nationwide antidrug advertising. The ONDCP and its partners ensured that the same energy and effort would be poured into education as a complementary element of the War on Drugs.

These drug education efforts were pervasive. They instilled fear in families and youngsters with heavy-handed messages about the effects of drugs and drug use. Much of the message was legitimate: messaging that talked about overdosing, addiction, health effects, and drugs' connection to gangs. Those messages also pushed ideas not well grounded in medical research, such as the ideas that marijuana is addictive like "hard" drugs and is a "gateway drug" inevitably leading to use of much more dangerous drugs.

Later, researchers attempted to evaluate the efficacy of these drug education programs. On its face, the "Just Say No" campaign was effective in rallying communities to come together and organize. In some sense, Nancy Reagan's call to arms synthesized efforts across the country to address youth drug use, but its actual effect seems to have been limited.[9] Communications scholars have also questioned the persuasiveness of such approaches, which might actually have the opposite of the intended effect (as the writers of the Eisenhower report had warned).

If the jury is out on the impact of abstinence advertising, the research is fairly clear on the effectiveness of the D.A.R.E. program—let's just say no. Multiple meta-analyses of existing research show that D.A.R.E. has little or no effect on youths' choices to experiment with drugs or to abstain. Much research also calls into question the D.A.R.E. program's worth in light of its tremendous cost.[10]

Thus, it can be said that the War on Drugs has not met expectations for any of its goals: combatting the flow of drugs into the United States, significantly reducing drug use, or having educational impact. Criminalization of drugs has filled America's prisons, but has done little to curb use and abuse rates. As for education and abstinence efforts, millions of students can consider themselves D.A.R.E. alums, but the evidence suggests the education efforts have had limited impact in achieving the drug war's aims.

BILL CLINTON'S DRUG WAR: A CHANGE IN TONE, NOT IN SUBSTANCE

Bill Clinton's election in 1992 ended twelve years of Republican control of the White House. Clinton was younger than his predecessors and had come of age in the 1960s. Clinton was also the first president in U.S. history to admit publicly to having tried marijuana. He spoke of drug policy with compassion, urging treatment for addicts and at times discussing drug use as a public health rather than as a public safety or law enforcement issue.

However, despite Clinton's kinder language about treatment, his policies still focused on criminalization and enforcement. Internationally this took the form of crop eradication efforts in Latin America, incentivizing those nations to destroy coca and cannabis crops and to crack down on production. Domestically crop eradication programs also continued.

Although efforts during the Clinton administration to expand treatment and reexamine sentencing guidelines were genuine, efforts to expand drug enforcement continued. In 1993, Executive Order No. 12880 elevated the director of the ONDCP to a cabinet-level position, and in President Clinton's second term, funding for that office and staff levels increased dramatically.

Any desires that Clinton had to scale back the drug war were hampered by high crime rates. Increases in crime, particularly violent crime, generated waves of fear across the country. That fear demanded a response from federal and state officials. Clinton's admission of having tried marijuana created pressure on him to clamp down strongly on crime, in part with antidrug policies. In the 1992 campaign, President George H. W. Bush had used Clinton's history to paint him as "soft on crime." As president, Clinton sought to shed that moniker. The capstone of that effort was the Violent Crime Control and Law Enforcement Act of 1994, commonly called the 1994 Crime Bill, signed into law by President Clinton in September 1994.[11]

Some of the provisions of the Crime Bill focused on prevention efforts among youth and treatment of drug-dependent users, yet the law also intensified criminalization.

It included a "three strikes" provision for violent criminals and traffickers, increases in funding for prisons, and a variety of grant programs for local law enforcement. Those law enforcement grants were distributed through the Byrne Program[12] (creating local drug taskforces), and developed the Community Oriented Policing Services (COPS) grant program within the Department of Justice. The COPS program funded large portions of the salaries of 100,000 police officers across the United States.

The 1994 Crime Bill helped extend a trend that had begun in 1991: dramatic annual increases in drug arrests.[13] There were approximately 327,000 marijuana arrests in 1991; by the end of the Clinton administration in 2000, that number had more than doubled, to over 700,000. Was the Crime Bill alone responsible for this increase? No—the trend had begun during the George H. W. Bush administration. However, that trend continued during the Clinton era and resulted in nearly three-quarters of a million marijuana arrests annually. At the same time, those who push back against criticism of federal marijuana arrests note that a large majority of those arrests take place at the state and local levels. However, the Crime Bill (and legislation earlier in the 1990s) served to facilitate state and local law enforcement agencies to have the manpower and resources to increase marijuana enforcement.

Another policy development that pushed the Clinton administration to take a hard line on marijuana was the state-level push to legalize medical marijuana. States began authorizing the production and use of medical marijuana starting the day President Clinton was reelected. Thus,

Clinton's desire to treat drug users ran up against states allowing the use of drugs for medical treatment. The administration response would serve as a new theater for Clinton's War on Drugs (the struggle to legalize medical marijuana is discussed in detail in chapter 11).

PART III **POT, THE PUBLIC, AND THE POWERFUL**

SEVEN DEMOGRAPHICS AND DEATH RESHAPE VIEWS ON MARIJUANA

IN A DEMOCRACY, public opinion is a powerful force. Americans both mock it and value it.

Some American presidents have been criticized for acting only in accordance with what the latest polls say, but when presidents advance policies that are at odds with the public, they are criticized for that, too. It can be unclear whether voters want their elected officials to be responsive to their interests or not, but for better or for worse, politicians are ever aware of polls. Serious missteps with key constituencies can quickly leave the commander-in-chief looking for a new job. Public opinion can help form and guide policy, particularly in an election year, or it can help maintain the status quo. Yet, public opinion is not static; it can be manipulated and moved. Eloquent or convincing advocates or officials, public experience, demographic shifts, and new information can sway public opinion. As can events.

Take for example, the events of September 11, 2001—a day that had an enormous effect on opinion. A poll of President George W. Bush's job approval from September 4 to September 6 found that 54 percent of Americans approved of the job the president was doing and 40 percent disapproved. Just thirty-two days later, a CBS News poll found Bush's approval rating at 90 percent; just 6 percent disapproved.[1] The latter results reflected what was widely seen as the president's effective response to the tragedy. Those events, among the most dramatic public opinion shocks in the history of polling, demonstrate the malleability of public opinion.

External events were not the only force acting on public opinion after 9/11. Tom Ridge, secretary of homeland security from 2003 to 2005, stated in 2009 that he was pressured to manipulate the color-coded terror threat level for political reasons, driving American attention back to terrorism and allowing President Bush to achieve his political and policy goals.[2] Clearly, elected and appointed officials have significant power to influence public views.

What is true of terrorism is also true of marijuana policy.

Throughout the first half of the twentieth century, most Americans had little contact with marijuana. It was not used recreationally by significant portions of the population, and most Americans had never tried it. In the early decades of the century it had been available as a medicine with a prescription, but as regulation and taxation increased, it was effectively and then formally outlawed.

Throughout this time, however, elected officials and political appointees, such as Harry Anslinger and well-known elites throughout the country, from Washington to Hollywood, portrayed drugs as a systemic menace. These forces used fearmongering and propaganda and coded racial language to convince Americans that drugs were like a disease infecting "good" communities and "innocent" people. And drugs were portrayed as an enemy that required a war to defeat.

This messaging from presidents and agencies with names that asserted both expertise and authority had an impact on public opinion. In fact, crafting public opinion on drug use and crime was central to Richard Nixon's electoral strategy: he recognized that if he could stoke fears among the public about the drug problem and then position himself as the individual most capable of fighting the war against drugs, he would benefit electorally. In many ways he was right.

MARIJUANA IS GROWING ON PEOPLE   In 1969, the Gallup Poll asked respondents whether they supported or opposed the legalization of marijuana. Only 12 percent of Americans supported legalization; 84 percent opposed it.[3] Those results reflected a nation fearful of marijuana's threat to the social fabric and unwilling to legalize.

What's more, there was little difference in public opinion among different demographic groups. Only 10 percent of women and 14 percent of men supported legalization. There were also very few differences by political affiliation: only 9 percent of Republicans, 12 percent of Democrats, and 14 percent of independents supported legalization.[4]

Politics helped set the stage for such low support for marijuana and that low support gave presidents and Congress the cover to expand the administrative apparatus of drug control over the course of decades. It amounted to a circular and reinforcing argument for prohibition. During the Nixon, Reagan, and Bush I administrations, the strategy of vilifying marijuana and marketing it to the American public as a threat and an enemy was effective at maintaining the status quo. For drug warriors, this was an ideal policy landscape.

Gallup and other polling organizations continued to ask respondents about marijuana legalization. Between 1969 and 1990 there were fluctuations in these polling results. Around the time Jimmy Carter was proposing marijuana decriminalization, support for legalization had grown to 30 percent, with only 66 percent opposing. That trend reversed during the 1980s as presidents once again used the apparatus of government to move public opinion away from Carter-era moderation back toward opposition. And twenty-one years after Gallup first asked respondents about marijuana legalization, support for it was statistically indistinguishable from when they first asked in 1969.[5]

Starting in the 1990s, however, opinions began to change. Support for legalization began to increase. By 2000, support for legalization jumped to 31 percent, and by 2013 a majority of Americans polled—as many as 58 percent—was supporting legalizing marijuana. These changes in poll results reflect a changing political and social landscape.

During the 1980s a combination of Reagan-era War on Drugs efforts and fear about rising crime rates likely reduced support for legalization from its late 1970s peak. This shift in opinion occurred because of both external events and the actions of thought leaders. Starting in the 1990s, the traditional War on Drugs effort, especially government advertising campaigns and other messaging, was starting to sound like a caricature of itself. Ultimately, "this is your brain on drugs"-style advertising evoked humor, rather than fear in the hearts and minds of many viewers. Demographics had an effect: the hippies got older and had their own families. State-level policies likely also induced polling shifts in the 1990s and 2000s. After California christened the medical marijuana movement in 1996, more states soon followed.

As Americans were exposed to functioning medical marijuana systems and eventually recreational marijuana systems, public opinion changed. Did legal marijuana cause a shift in public opinion, or vice versa? Very likely existing medical marijuana systems helped shift an already moving public opinion (the trend began years before the first medical marijuana system was established), and that shifting public opinion, in turn, generated the support necessary to pass ballot initiatives in other states.

Actual events around the country are likely only part of the explanation for the dramatic shifts in opinion. What demographers call generational replacement is another: quite simply, some people die and other people turn eighteen (affecting the pool of both poll respondents and voters). On some issues, that kind of generational replacement matters little. For marijuana policy, the impact was profound. In 1969, the polled groups included those born between 1900 and 1924 (the greatest generation) and those born between 1925 and 1945 (the silent generation).

Only 7 percent of the greatest generation supported legalization, while 15 percent of the silent generation did.

By 1990 Gallup's respondents included members of four generations: the greatest, the silent, the baby boomers (born between 1946 and 1964), and some generation-Xers (born 1965 to 1980). This poll shows very little changing of minds among the first two groups (the greatest generation, 12 percent support; the silent generation, 14 percent). But 17 percent of baby boomers and 21 percent of gen-Xers supported marijuana legalization, raising the poll's final result to 16 percent for legalization. It is clear that younger Americans offered higher levels of support than their parents and grandparents.

By 2000 differences among those age groups' opinions had been magnified in poll results as support nationally stood at 31 percent. By this time, the greatest generation had largely "exited the electorate"—died off and composed a very small subset of the sample. Thus, the age cohort had a significantly lower impact on aggregate public opinion. The 2000 Gallup poll's sample was dominated by members of the silent generation, baby boomers, and gen-Xers.[6] Three forces in play put significant upward pressure on the overall nationwide support for marijuana legalization: generational replacement, changing opinion, and the composition of the poll sample. The silent generation supported legalization at a rate of 23 percent, up nine percentage points in ten years. Baby boomers also increased their support for marijuana legalization to 30 percent, from 17 percent in 1990. The most dramatic increase came from gen-Xers, which went from 21 percent in support of marijuana legalization to 41 percent in 2000. But in 1990 not all gen-Xers were of voting age; only those born between

1965 and 1972 would have been included in the poll. By 2000, all gen-Xers were of voting age, ensuring gen-Xers made up a significantly larger share of the overall sample in 2000 than in 1990. Second, their absolute support (41 percent) was significantly higher than that of any other age demographic. Third, gen-Xers' support for marijuana legalization increased significantly between 1990 and 2000.

Over time, and particularly after 1990, support for marijuana legalization grew quite rapidly. By the 2015 poll, millennials were included in the sample and their support stood at 71 percent. Yet experience also mattered. People who experimented with marijuana—and an increasing share of the population was doing so—saw that they did not automatically become schizophrenic sexual predators intent on committing acts of murder, nor did they necessarily drop out of college and forego a life of success or inexorably become attracted and addicted to hard drugs. Their experience with the drug was far less harmful than government rhetoric and advertising had been warning for decades. The same experience dynamic applied as states began implementing medical marijuana regimes: the sky didn't fall.

Differences among age cohorts are not the only divisions in the population when it comes to legalizing marijuana. Gallup and Pew have both found significant differences based on party affiliation. A 2013 Gallup poll and a 2015 Pew poll both found tepid support for legalization among Republicans (Gallup: 35 percent; Pew: 39 percent), whereas both independents' and Democrats' was clearly stronger. Independents' support level (Gallup: 62 percent; Pew: 58 percent) is virtually indistinguishable from Democrats' (Gallup: 65 percent; Pew: 59).[7]

There are also differences, albeit smaller, between men's and women's support (57 versus to 49 percent) and between whites and African Americans (55 versus 58 percent); support among Latinos (40 percent) is significantly lower.[8] It is clear that not everyone agrees on legalization and that some groups are quite wary of legalization. Overall, however, polling results show that Americans are becoming increasingly comfortable with and supportive of scrapping prohibition and trying out a new system to govern and regulate marijuana in the United States.

OTHER SUPPORT FOR MARIJUANA   We can also look elsewhere to get perspective on the strength of support for marijuana reform. One place to look is the issue of medical marijuana, which by 2016 had become widespread policy in the United States. By mid-2016, twenty-five states and the District of Columbia reformed laws to authorize a full-fledged medical marijuana program. Eighteen states joined California in setting up medical marijuana systems before Colorado and Washington became the nation's first states to approve recreational legalization in 2012.[9] A 1999 Gallup poll showed robust support for medical marijuana: 73 percent for and only 25 percent opposed. Between 1999 and 2010, Gallup polls have shown support fluctuating between 70 and 78 percent, with opposition never rising above 27 percent (in 2010).[10]

CBS News was among the first of several polling organizations that began asking about medical marijuana. The CBS poll asked respondents: "Do you think doctors should be allowed to prescribe small amounts of marijuana for patients suffering from serious illnesses, or not?"[11] When CBS conducted the poll in 2012, support for medical marijuana was 83 percent for, with only 13 percent against. Support peaked at 86 percent in CBS's 2014 poll, then fell to 83 percent in 2015.[12]

National polls notwithstanding, federal law still declares medical marijuana to be illegal. The reforms are happening at the state level. Since 2000, several state legislatures have approved medical marijuana programs—these states tend to be ones with no or very limited ballot initiative procedures. Those states, like Connecticut, Delaware, Maryland, and New York (to name a few), tend to be heavily Democratic states, with a few exceptions (such as Ohio). That those laws have not been reversed does not necessarily illustrate widespread support, but at least suggests a lack of passionate opposition. In addition, since 1996 about a dozen states have passed ballot initiatives approving medical marijuana. The success of those initiatives indicates that at least a majority of voters are supportive.[13] These states include traditionally blue (Democratic-voting) states such as California and Massachusetts, traditionally red (Republican-voting) states like Montana and Alaska, and purple (swing) states such as Colorado and Nevada.

Many of the remaining nonmedical marijuana states are among the nation's most conservative states. Yet even in these states, polls suggest there is substantial support for reforming medical marijuana laws. A roundup of polling from the Marijuana Policy Project shows that even in the Bible Belt, support for medical marijuana is quite robust: 75 percent in Alabama, 80 percent in Georgia, 71 percent in Oklahoma, 58 percent in Texas.[14] Among more politically moderate states support is even higher: 76 percent in Wisconsin, and 87 percent in Iowa.[15]

JUST HOW POPULAR IS MARIJUANA REFORM?   Support for medical marijuana reform is not scattered among liberal strongholds or libertarian states; support is ubiquitous. Do these high levels of support for legalizing medical marijuana provide evidence of a dramatic shift in America's views toward drugs more generally? Is public support for marijuana a proxy for relaxed views about substances the government deems dangerous and renders illegal?

One of the arguments often mounted against marijuana legalization is that it creates a slippery slope—one that may lead to large-scale drug decriminalization or legalization of a panoply of illegal substances. A poll conducted by Huffington Post and YouGov in 2014 asked respondents whether they support or oppose the legalization of marijuana and a variety of other substances. This poll is quite important in the drug reform debate. Fifty-one percent of respondents supported legalizing marijuana, and 34 percent opposed. Public opinion was starkly different for other substances, however. Only 11 percent of respondents wanted to legalize cocaine, whereas 83 percent wanted to keep it illegal. Similarly, crack cocaine, heroin, and LSD all had levels of support in the single digits, with opposition to legalization over 80 percent in each case. The Huffington Post–YouGov poll illustrates that while public views on marijuana have clearly relaxed and shifted toward legalization, Americans are far from being on any kind of slippery slope.

Public perception in the United States is that marijuana policies—and only marijuana policies—are in need of reform. Americans are exceptionally resistant to the idea of legalizing any other drugs currently considered dangerous by the government and associated with criminal activity.

Another way to put support for marijuana into perspective is to compare support for legalization of marijuana with other measures of support in American society. The October 2015 Gallup poll estimate of support for marijuana legalization was 58 percent. President Obama has reached 58 percent job approval in only one poll since 2010.[16] Throughout most of his second term, his job approval has been below 50 percent. The last time Congress had an approval rating of 58 percent was April 2002, in the aftermath of the September 11 terror attacks and in the midst of the war in Afghanistan.[17] Other than immediately post-9/11, Gallup has not registered support for Congress above 57 percent since they started asking the question in 1974.[18] The 2015 level of support for marijuana legalization is about the same as public support for the United States Supreme Court—support for the Court has never polled higher than 62 percent.[19]

Gallup asks respondents to express their confidence level in a variety of American institutions with "a great deal," "quite a lot," "some," or "very little." Gallup defines "confidence" by the percentage of respondents who say "a great deal" or "quite a lot." By that metric, support for marijuana legalization is higher than American confidence in the police, organized religion, the medical system, the presidency, the public schools, banks, organized labor, newspapers, the criminal justice system, television news, and big business.[20]

EIGHT CANNABIS USE AS A LIFESTYLE OF THE RICH AND FAMOUS

DURING MUCH OF THE twentieth century cannabis in all its forms and uses was pushed to the fringes of society, its production and use associated with crime and delinquency. Taboos on the use of cannabis for any purpose kept most people in the dark as to the plant's true value. Despite the forces of prohibition working to distance people from pot, America has a long relationship with the cannabis plant and the use of marijuana. Some of America's most famous and most powerful historical figures have played an important role in marijuana's presence in the United States. Highlighting those roles helps illustrate how mainstream the plant has been since before the Revolution and how prevalent the cultivation and use of marijuana has actually been.

CANNABIS CULTIVATORS WE ALL KNOW With so many states legalizing recreational or medical marijuana or both, and a
number of states permitting home growing, cultivating
marijuana has become quite common. Twenty-first-century
cannabis cultivation occurs in hobbyists' plots, massive
outdoor farms, sizable multifloor indoor grow operations,
and walled-off outdoor gardens—and there even are corporate agribusiness marijuana operations.

This new visibility notwithstanding, cannabis cultivation actually has a long history in North America, dating
back to the Colonial era. Hemp was a critical crop in the
colonies, and some of America's most revered historical
figures and other lesser-known individuals have had an
outsized impact on production. In Jamestown, Virginia,
growing cannabis for hemp-based products was man-
dated by the British Crown. Later, Colonial governments
in Massachusetts and Virginia required land-owning
farmers to grow it. George Washington and Thomas Jefferson were well-known, successful hemp farmers who
noted in their journals the precise processes by which they
farmed the crop.[1] In Massachusetts, John Adams, too,
grew hemp, writing (under a pseudonym) of "hemp's
mind-altering capabilities."[2] Farmers across the young
United States grew hemp for personal use; as a cash crop
for the production of textiles, ropes for sea vessels, food,
and oil; and, surely, as the future president John Adams
pointed out, for occasional recreational use.

A contemporary grower whose name is not a household
one has a grow operation that may be one of the most interesting anywhere. Dr. Mahmoud ElSohly, research professor at the Research Institute of Pharmaceutical Sciences

at the University of Mississippi, is the federal government's pot supplier. Since the late 1960s, Ole Miss has been awarded a series of contracts from the National Institute on Drug Abuse (NIDA) to produce, study, and distribute marijuana for research and as part of the federal government's Compassionate Investigational New Drug (IND) program. He maintains the cannabis research portion of the university's National Center for Natural Products Research. The contract with NIDA was renewed in 2015 to the tune of nearly $69 million to support the twelve-acre facility and thousand-square-foot indoor grow.[3] The U.S. government needs weed for a variety of reasons—primarily to provide a reliable, consistent product for research—and Dr. ElSohly is paid to provide it.

ElSohly's role is relatively unknown, but some celebrities have become part of the cannabis industry. Recognizing the opportunities that a blossoming legal market provides, some ardent supporters of marijuana use and legalization have lent their name—their "brand"—to marijuana enterprise. They may not be tilling a field, but they are surely planting the seed in the minds of consumers that the products they endorse are worth the purchase. Snoop Dogg's "Leafs by Snoop" brand offers a variety of marijuana flower and edibles; Willie Nelson's "Willie's Reserve" brand provides tins of marijuana flower; the family of the late Bob Marley has allowed a company, Privateer Holdings, to develop the brand Marley Natural.

MARIJUANA AND POPULAR MUSIC Speaking of Marley, Willie, and Snoop, marijuana has long been the drug of choice among the world's most famous musicians and singers.

Marijuana is not just a source of creativity, not just a substance that musicians claim opens minds and helps them write songs. Marijuana is also a muse mentioned by name or allusion in the lyrics of hundreds of songs. And it's not just a recent phenomenon, although Halsey's 2015 hit "New Americana" may be among the first to include a line about being "high on legal marijuana." The tradition has been around for nearly a century. Louis Armstrong in the late 1920s played "Muggles," a slang jazz and blues term for marijuana. A few years later, Cab Calloway sang "Reefer Man," a bold title for a 1932 song at a time when marijuana prohibition efforts were being ratcheted up.

Those early works foreshadowed decades of music about marijuana and the fusion of marijuana and musical identity which was a huge part of a generation's popular music. Artists of the 1960s and 1970s both credited marijuana as a creative spark and sang about it explicitly, for example Bob Marley's song "Kaya," the Beatles' "Got to Get You into My Life," and Bob Dylan's "Rainy Day Women," which declared, "Everybody must get stoned." For fans of bands such as Phish and the Grateful Dead, getting high on pot became a communal ritual that was an essential, almost Eucharistic, part of their musical experience. Pot and being high was a staple subject of songs in almost every pop genre: reggae, hip-hop, grunge, punk, and hard rock.

MARIJUANA AND THE MOVIES Movie and TV celebrities have been known to dabble with pot, too, and as with music, it's not just a recent trend. Marijuana was no stranger to Hollywood's Golden Age. Groucho Marx famously admitted to consuming marijuana repeatedly over the course of a month—although he blamed it on frequent accidental ingestion. Thomas McNulty, in his 2011 biography of Errol Flynn, notes that the actor admitted to using marijuana, among a host of other drugs. One of the highest-profile actors of the day to be known to have used marijuana was Robert Mitchum. In 1948 he was arrested for marijuana possession, ultimately serving time for the crime at a California prison camp.[4] Marx, Flynn, and Mitchum were among the many early stars to be associated with marijuana, but they surely would not be the last.

It would be pointless, if not impossible, to assemble a list of big- and small-screen stars who have admitted to using marijuana. However, there are a few important points to note in the evolution of marijuana and the cultural context. Nowadays Hollywood thinks nothing of a celebrity's using or admitting to have used marijuana, but it was not always like that. During the 1930s and 1940s, Hollywood executives were stridently opposed to the product and actively sought to combat it. Mitchum's arrest in 1948 was part of a sting operation coordinated to catch high-profile marijuana users. It was Hollywood executives who produced and/or pushed propagandistic films such as *Marihuana* (1936) and, perhaps most infamously, *Reefer Madness* (1937). These films are now cult favorites for their over-the-top treatment of the drug. Viewers now watch the films to laugh, as they have become comedic caricatures of cannabis anxiety, but at the time of their release they were intended as serious educational tools to incite fear among Americans.

Over time, Hollywood changed, as did the portrayal of marijuana in movies. It could have come as a result of a changing of the guard in Tinseltown, where more moderate producers, directors, and executives replaced the prohibitionists. The change may have come in response to marijuana's rise in popularity throughout the 1960s not simply as a product to get you high, but as a meaningful cultural element signifying a multitude of emotions and ideas. The change may have come simply as a market force, as the children of the 1960s were ready, willing, and eager to see their generation portrayed in realistic light, rather than with an antiseptic wash of a drug-free America. More likely the change happened because of some combination of the three.

Regardless of the cause, Hollywood began to accept and eventually embrace marijuana as part of the script of life. In the 1970s, comedians Cheech Marin and Tommy Chong pushed the envelope, starring in a series of Cheech & Chong movies that thrust marijuana into the mainstream. The films didn't glorify marijuana use—few aspired to be like Cheech. But they did show marijuana as something to laugh at, rather than the substance liable to make society collapse. The Cheech & Chong series launched a cottage industry in films in which marijuana played supporting or even leading roles. The 1980s saw films with brief stints of marijuana use, like *The Breakfast Club* (1985), but the 1990s and 2000s produced films in which marijuana was the star. *Dazed and Confused* (1993) and *Half Baked* (1998) made stars out of the comedians Dave Chappelle, Ben Affleck, and Matthew McConaughey. In the 2000s, entire film series, for example, *Jay and Silent Bob* and *Harold and Kumar,* focused on frequent marijuana use. Although, as some of the titles suggest, these films typically featured younger burned-out characters, they were still important in highlighting a transition in Hollywood attitudes toward pot in ways that challenged taboos and took marijuana more mainstream.

The content of films was not the only important way in which actors embraced marijuana. Some celebrities have openly spoken about their use of medical marijuana and the benefits they have found from it. Montel Williams was among one of the first celebrities to discuss his use of marijuana for therapeutic purposes. In 1999 he was diagnosed with multiple sclerosis; shortly thereafter he started a treatment that included marijuana. He has noted that it helps him with pain relief and as a sleep aid.[5] His experience has made him an outspoken advocate on behalf of reform, even lobbying the Pennsylvania legislature to pass a medical marijuana law in 2015, reform that ultimately passed in 2016.

The singer Melissa Etheridge has also spoken openly about her use of marijuana as she battled breast cancer, about how cannabis helped mitigate the side effects of chemotherapy. Whoopi Goldberg has discussed her use of medical marijuana to diminish the ocular pressure she suffers as a glaucoma patient. In fact, in March 2016, Goldberg took the leap from patient to entrepreneur, announcing the opening of Whoopi & Maya, a medical cannabis company offering products specifically geared toward women's health.

CANNABIS AND CORPORATE AMERICA   One concern that opponents of marijuana reform often raise is the cognitive decline marijuana users *do* suffer in the short and long term. Legitimate research suggests that many of those concerns are exaggerated, but the image of burned-out stoners suffering couchlock, beholden to the munchies, unemployed, and living with their parents has cultural resonance. This image has been reinforced not only by some of the government advertising discussed in chapter 6 but also by some of the films just mentioned.

The idea that marijuana ruins lives, turning young people from a life of productivity to a life of mediocrity, has taken hold in some quarters. There is, however, a group of people who push back against that notion, who defy the commonly held stereotype of unproductive lives led in a haze of marijuana smoke. Those people are among the world's most successful businessmen.

Among their ranks are not just young millennials who struck it rich founding social media platforms but also some of the nation's—the world's—wealthiest entrepreneurs. People such as financier George Soros has said he's used marijuana on his way to building one of the most successful financial empires in the world. Richard Branson—wealthy, successful, and a leader in the aviation industry—admits to smoking pot.[6] The former CEO of Men's Wearhouse, George Zimmer, is not shy about being a regular marijuana user and has contributed money to the cause of legalizing marijuana.[7] Even Michael Bloomberg—billionaire, corporate executive, and the former mayor of New York City—despite having a mixed record on marijuana policy, has admitted he used marijuana and liked it.[8]

Marijuana use isn't the path to inventing the next game-changing technology, nor is it a sure way to make billions of dollars. But what these business leaders do show is that using marijuana doesn't prevent an individual from leading a successful life. Instead, they demonstrate that American society has progressed to a point where a CEO's admission of marijuana use does not damage his personal or business reputation.

POT AND POLITICS: AN EVER-EVOLVING RELATIONSHIP

Marijuana is no stranger to politics. Political figures' relationship with marijuana, in the United States and abroad, is fascinating and tells us much about changes in society and culture. There is a deep irony inherent in politicians, elected leaders, and government officials using marijuana: government is the source of prohibition. Alas, government hypocrisy is nothing new, and it certainly seeps into marijuana policy.

Government officials have long used cannabis plants for various purposes, including getting high. Many of the nation's Founding Fathers grew and profited from hemp. Historically in Chinese culture, cannabis was used frequently for medicinal purposes even by the nation's emperors. Some Persian cultures used cannabis products and its seeds for a variety of purposes. England's Henry VIII and his daughter, Elizabeth I, both issued decrees requiring the growth of cannabis among British farmers for the production of hemp.[9] Later, Queen Victoria was prescribed medical marijuana by the royal physician as a pain reliever for menstrual cramps. At that time the use of cannabis as medicine was lawful in Britain, and not uncommon.

During 150 years or so of U.S. history, cannabis was used for medicinal purposes in a variety of ways. Hemp and even psychoactive marijuana was grown legally throughout the states, and doctors used some of the harvest in their practices. Early regulations simply put restrictions on the prescription of cannabis. It is almost certain that, along the way, some elected officials were prescribed cannabis-based medicines for treatment.

During marijuana prohibition, the use of the product became so taboo, such a liability, that politicians likely carefully concealed any use of marijuana to protect their reputations and political prospects. One of the first cannabis controversies involving a high-profile elected official occurred in 1978 and involved U.S. Congressman Ned Pattison (D-N.Y.). He admitted to smoking marijuana occasionally. The issue, which emerged in the course of his campaign for a third term, ultimately doomed him, and on Election Day, 1978, voters of New York's 29th district elected his Republican opponent.

One of the more high-profile political scandals involving marijuana occurred nine years later, in a bizarre turn of events concerning the nomination of a Supreme Court justice. In June 1987, Lewis Powell, associate justice of the Supreme Court, retired. President Reagan initially nominated U.S. Court of Appeals Judge Robert Bork to replace Powell, but Bork's controversial positions and statements ultimately led the U.S. Senate to reject him. On October 29, 1987, President Reagan nominated one of Bork's Appeals Court colleagues, forty-one-year old Douglas Ginsburg.

In his nomination speech, Reagan noted the importance of Ginsburg's nomination and the need for a speedy confirmation. He argued that since the Powell retirement, "The empty seat on the Supreme Court has been a casualty in the fight for victims' rights and the war against crime."[10] Within days, however, controversy arose. National Public Radio's Nina Totenberg reported that Ginsburg had smoked marijuana, not just as a youth but when he was an assistant professor at Harvard Law School. That sounded a death knell for Ginsburg's nomination. Not only was he being asked to serve on the Court to be tough on crime, but Reagan's own prosecution of the War on Drugs raised the risk of his appearing hypocritical if he pursued the Ginsburg nomination.

Less than two weeks after he had been nominated, Ginsburg withdrew his nomination. Ultimately, Anthony Kennedy was nominated and confirmed. Seventeen years after taking his seat on the Court, Kennedy's turned out to be one of the pivotal votes in *Gonzales v. Raich,* which ruled that the federal government could continue to arrest people on marijuana charges, even when they are complying with state medical marijuana laws.

The aftermath of the failed Ginsburg nomination provided more interesting developments. Although Ginsburg's admitted marijuana use was too offensive for President Reagan, the media, and the establishment of both political parties to allow him to take a seat on the highest court in the land, he retained his seat as a judge on the D.C. Circuit of the U.S. Court of Appeals, a court that has often been nicknamed the second-highest court in the land. Apparently, in 1987 marijuana use was only controversial enough to bar nominees from the Supreme Court.

Ginsburg's admission prompted other public officials to admit to having used marijuana. Two 1988 presidential candidates, Al Gore (D-Tenn.) and Bruce Babbitt (D-Ariz.), both admitted to having used marijuana when they were younger. In fact, Gore mentioned that he and his wife, Tipper, both did. Senator Claiborne Pell (D-R.I.) and the future Speaker of the House Newt Gingrich (R-Ga.) both admitted to having tried marijuana in their youth.[11]

Thus the Ginsburg nomination led to a more open discussion of marijuana, so that marijuana use—almost always framed at the time as an embarrassing, regrettable, youthful indiscretion—could now be mentioned even in the highest levels of politics. Presidential candidates and senior members of Congress could admit that they used marijuana—so long as they didn't use it too often—and not be ostracized. Gore and Babbitt failed to get their party's nomination in 1988, but the reasons had nothing to do with their admitted marijuana use. Senator Pell was reelected to a sixth term after his confession. Gingrich went on to be reelected six more times, and become Speaker of the House in 1995. The years 1987 and 1988 marked the beginning of a transition in American politics in which the taboo topic of marijuana became ever so slightly more acceptable to discuss, within specific bounds.

Marijuana would continue to be a factor in later presidential campaigns, especially as children of the sixties, began running for president. In 1992, the Democratic nominee for president, Bill Clinton, sheepishly admitted to having tried marijuana as a Rhodes Scholar, with the caveat that he "didn't inhale." The Clinton campaign was facing a steady flow of questions about his character, and President George H. W. Bush was mounting an all-out offensive to convince American voters that Bill Clinton was not the type of person who should occupy the White House. Despite his admission, Clinton went on to win that November. He became the first individual to admit to having used marijuana and win the presidency. Of course, he would not be the last.

After George W. Bush had dodged the question on the campaign trail, he admitted to having used marijuana as a youth. Again the worry was that his admission would be seen as a liability to his gravitas and even an invitation for contemporary youths to follow his example. At least Bush admitted he had inhaled, and by the time the information came to light, the American public thought little of it. Then, in the 2008 election, when Barack Obama became the first African American nominee for president, the marijuana taboo was deconstructed a bit more. Throughout the nomination and especially the general election campaign, racially tinged challenges and questions flung at him ranged from his place of birth to the company he kept at church to his time living abroad to his substance use.

In his 1995 memoir, *Dreams of My Father,* Obama admits having smoking marijuana and even doing cocaine as a young man. Later, as he was mulling over making a bid for the presidency, members of the media began asking about that admission. In a quip and a clear reference to President Clinton's less-than-convincing response, Obama bluntly stated, "When I was a kid, I inhaled. That was the point."[12] This response and that open discussion of drug use caused little fanfare. Obama went on to be elected and reelected president, and his prior drug use clearly did little to hinder his success. However, had he been arrested while possessing or using marijuana or cocaine, he likely would never have had the opportunities that positioned him to run for the Senate and eventually to be elected president. Fortunately for him he had a clean criminal record and could reflect upon his drug use later in life with few if any negative repercussions.

THE 2016 PRESIDENTIAL CAMPAIGN AND A NEW ERA IN POT POLITICS

The 2016 presidential race was among the most interesting in modern memory. The race began with nearly two dozen candidates vying for their respective parties' nominations: five Democrats and seventeen Republicans. Political novices emerged as powerful forces within the contest, channeling voters' anger and interest in seeing something new.

But beyond the candidates, something else was quite new about 2016: how candidates engaged with marijuana policy. Most of the candidates who admitted having used marijuana offered the same standard, milquetoast lines about youthful indiscretions, experimentation, regret, and the implicit or explicit warning like that a typical sitcom dad might give: "My doing this doesn't mean it's okay for you to do it." The sheer number of candidates who admitted to using pot or at least trying it—seven— was a bit or a surprise. A handful said they never had used pot and another handful refused to say one way or the other or were never pointedly asked. Regardless of the numbers and the words used, the discussion of personal use was not a "gotcha" moment with the power to doom a candidacy; the questions were evidence more of curiosity and perhaps a desire to establish whether a candidate's position on marijuana matched his or her behaviors.

No candidate was obliged to withdraw from the race after admitting he had smoked pot. Some candidates, like former Florida governor Jeb Bush, noticeably squirmed before relenting with their confessions and offering their contrition; their past marijuana use was ultimately a non-issue. But that doesn't mean marijuana policy wasn't an issue in the campaigns. To the contrary, marijuana policy questions came up in debates, in questions from voters, and in media interviews. As the United States—or at least individual states—continued down the path of reform, the electorate's interest in marijuana policy was strong. Candidates were asked about how they would handle marijuana policy as president. The responses varied, but what was most interesting was the fact that there were responses. There were plans and proposals. Candidates set themselves apart from each other and apart from the president. Some showed nuanced knowledge about particulars of policy and the levers of government that needed to be pulled in order to enact the change they advocated.

The positions ran the gambit from ardent prohibition to substantial reform. Governor Chris Christie (R-N.J.) may well have been the field's most staunch drug warrior. As a former federal prosecutor, he condemned the Obama administration's hands-off approach (use of enforcement discretion) to look the other way on legalized, recreational marijuana. Christie argued that he would enforce the Controlled Substances Act everywhere, implying that he would shut down state-legal systems. However, even Christie suggested that he would allow medical marijuana systems to continue to operate, even though they, too, violate the same federal laws. That distinction likely reflects Christie's recognition of the substantial support nationwide and in the states for medical marijuana—support even a committed prohibitionist must bend to.

Many of the other 2016 presidential candidates offered some version of reform as an alternative to the prohibition status quo; still others stayed quite tight-lipped on the issue. Governor John Kasich of Ohio found himself in an interesting position in late 2015. While running for president, his state voted on a legalization ballot initiative. Kasich opposed the measure, but was able to keep the discussion of marijuana policy focused solely on the shortcomings and problems of the specific Ohio ballot measure, rather than being forced to enter into a broader discussion about marijuana legalization. After withdrawing from the presidential race, Kasich would go on to sign legislation in June 2016 authorizing a full medical marijuana program in Ohio.

Former secretary of state Hillary Clinton, the Democratic nominee, offered positions and proposals. Although she stated that she opposed legalizing recreational marijuana nationwide, she indicated that she supported medical marijuana programs and would even acquiesce in states' choices as to whether to legalize recreational marijuana for their residents. She argued that the federal government should not be in the business of shutting down functional, state-legal programs. In addition, she supported moving marijuana from its status as a Schedule I substance to the next-lower tier, Schedule II, in an effort to encourage research and increase knowledge.

Senator Rand Paul (R-Ky.), a physician, was among the most pro-reform candidates in the 2016 race—in fact, in the entire U.S. Senate. He spoke passionately about freedom, criminal justice, and government spending as issues involved in the marijuana debate. He spoke about racial disparities in arrests and the consequences of that reality.

He advocated for marijuana policy reform in line with his sponsorship of a 2015 bill called the Compassionate Access, Research Expansion, and Respect States Act (CARERS). CARERS is comprehensive legislation that would reschedule marijuana, expand research opportunities, broaden access to medical marijuana for veterans, and permit states to develop medical marijuana programs and still be in compliance with federal law. CARERS was the most detailed marijuana legislation proposed in the U.S. Senate in American history and was the most thoughtful proposal unveiled by any of the candidates on the 2016 campaign trail. With CARERS, Paul showed marijuana to be a complex, challenging public policy in serious need of a fix—a fix at least one presidential candidate was willing to make.

The policy recommendations of Senator Bernie Sanders, the independent senator from Vermont who unsuccessfully sought the Democratic presidential nomination, evolved during the campaign season. Ultimately he proposed the most extreme changes in marijuana policy of any candidate, presenting new legislation in the Senate whereby marijuana would be removed from the Controlled Substances Act schedules entirely and instead would be regulated more like alcohol or tobacco than like a narcotic.

Campaign 2016 was the first presidential race in which marijuana reform was treated as a legitimate, serious public policy issue. It was important enough so that those vying to be president of the United States not only were asked about their history with the drug but also were expected to develop policy. For the reform movement, this was a tremendous victory for their cause. Marijuana was not being discussed as a joke nor introduced as an effort to corner a candidate in a scandal. It was not a taboo topic that only fringe candidates would engage. It was an issue being addressed by front-runners and candidates up and down the polls. By 2016, marijuana was mainstream in a national election.

PART IV **MARIJUANA REFORM BLOSSOMS INTO PUBLIC POLICY**

NINE DECRIMINALIZATION AS THE FIRST RETREAT FROM PROHIBITION

IN WASHINGTON, D.C., a War on Drugs had been launched, and a series of presidents and congressional majorities continued to crack down on all drugs, including marijuana. But in the states the mood, and the attitude, was different. In response to the 1972 Shafer report, initially commissioned by President Richard Nixon and then later criticized and ignored by him, the states had begun to consider their own marijuana laws. The Shafer report had criticized marijuana prohibition and recommended decriminalization rather than legalization as an effective policy change. In the states people paid attention to these recommendations, particularly during periods of budget shortfalls, because they recognized that law enforcement resources were targeting low-level, nonviolent marijuana offenses instead of more serious drug crimes.

In 1973, Oregon passed the nation's first marijuana decriminalization legislation, which removed criminal penalties for low-level possession. Rather than being arrested, booked, and tried, those caught with small amounts of marijuana would receive the equivalent of a traffic ticket and fine. Other states followed suit, including Alaska, Maine, Colorado, California, and Ohio in 1975; Minnesota in 1976; Mississippi, New York, and North Carolina in 1977; and Nebraska in 1978.[1] As this movement progressed, decriminalization gained backing even from the Carter White House.

Many of the decriminalization measures functioned similarly. They removed what were typically misdemeanor charges for simple possession. Those misdemeanor charges were meaningful because they led to an arrest and conviction and a criminal record that was often permanent. Typically the fine was $100 (the Shafer report's recommendation) and commonly applied to possession of one ounce of marijuana or less (another Schafer recommendation). In several of the states, that reduced penalty would apply only for one's first offense. Subsequent offenses were not afforded such leniency, though some states, including Alaska, did not restrict leniency to the first offense.

In 1978 Nebraska decriminalized, the last state to do so for a while. The energy died down, as a new president was elected in 1980 and the Shafer report became a distant memory. The drive for reform gave way to a rush for war.

Not until the 2000s—when states began legalizing medical and then recreational marijuana—would new life be breathed into the decriminalization movement. Those legal reforms coincided with rapidly changing public opinion in a population that wanted to see law enforcement resources spent on something other than arresting thousands of American youths every year. Those policy changes came as a result of ballot initiatives and state legislative action. Between 2008 and 2016, no fewer than eleven states passed formal decriminalization measures. Four more and the District of Columbia actually legalized marijuana. These moves dramatically changed the marijuana policy landscape in the United States.

In the 1970s, as in the 2000s, there were many reasons for decriminalizing marijuana. First, it removed the prospect of prison for those caught with small amounts of marijuana—a penalty that existed in some jurisdictions and one that many felt to be too severe. Second, it ensured that individuals—especially younger people and people of color—would not automatically have a criminal record that could prevent future opportunities in employment and education. Third, it still maintained a fine, signaling official disapproval of drug use and maintaining a source of revenue for the government.

But decriminalization still is problematic.

- Employers in many states can still ask prospective employees about marijuana citations (if not about arrests) and judge them accordingly even in the absence of a criminal record.
- Under decriminalization, the production and distribution of marijuana is still outlawed. That means any individual who desires marijuana must still procure that product from an unregulated illegal market.

- Decriminalization may affect the marijuana consumer, but does nothing to change the landscape surrounding marijuana producers.
- Evidence from Vermont suggests that under the state's decriminalization statute, the number of citations being issued was significantly higher than the number of arrests before decriminalization. Although this phenomenon is not occurring in all decriminalization states, it does suggest that in some jurisdictions, police may prefer the streamlined process of marijuana citations (involving less paperwork than a formal arrest) and actually enforce the law more aggressively.

For reform activists, decriminalization is an improvement over drug war–style hypercriminalization, but it is not a comprehensive solution to the inequities that result from the ways marijuana laws are actually enforced. Thus, decriminalization was just a first step in the drug reform movement; it would be succeeded by broader, more comprehensive reforms that met more of the advocacy community's demands.

TEN GANJA GRIDLOCK

The Failures of Federal Reform

WHEREAS DECRIMINALIZATION REFORMS succeeded in many states, decriminalization failed at the federal level. However, decriminalization efforts were not the only reforms that were proposed for the federal level. Starting in the early 1970s, two routes were attempted to reform federal marijuana laws, one route dependent on congressional action and the other requiring administrative action. By and large, these efforts turned out to be fruitless until the mid-2010s.

REFORMS CENTERED IN CONGRESS Congress has looked at a variety of pieces of legislation intended to reevaluate or rewrite the nation's marijuana laws. As far back as the Ninety-Third Congress (January 1973 to January 1975),

shortly after the passage of the CSA, legislators began filing marijuana reform bills. At the start of that Congress,
Representative Ed Koch (D-N.Y.) introduced H.R. 669,
"A bill to amend certain provisions of the Controlled Substances Act relating to marijuana." This bill, which Koch
proposed multiple times during that Congress, would
make it "not unlawful" to possess marijuana for personal
use in one's dwelling or in public nor would it be unlawful
to "distribute, transfer or sell, in public or private," so
long as the exchange was not made for profit. These bills
were somewhat similar to decriminalization legislation,
but they did not specify a fine, nor consider possession an
offense. Instead Koch's bill simply declares that an individual possessing a personal amount of marijuana (no amount
specified) would not be violating the Controlled Substances
Act. Unlike decriminalization, Koch's bill would essentially
legalize the possession and sale of small amounts of marijuana. A few weeks later, Senator Jacob Javits (R-N.Y.)
introduced S. 746, a bill nearly identical to Koch's.

On December 14, 1973, Congressman Sam Young
(R-Ill.) introduced H.R. 11981, "A bill to amend the
Controlled Substances Act to permit the referral to drug
counseling or treatment programs of certain first-time
marijuana offenders and to remove certain age restrictions against the expunging of certain official records."
The title of the bill stated Young's intentions. It neither
legalized nor decriminalized marijuana but instead offered alternative sentences (probation including drug
treatment) in lieu of jail time for certain first-time marijuana offenders. It also relaxed expunging requirements
for records. This legislation didn't remove the criminality

of the behavior but reformed the punishment convicted individuals would face.

As mentioned in chapter 8, much of the marijuana reform legislation during the rest of the 1970s focused on decriminalization, usually attaching a $100 fine for simple possession of small amounts of marijuana. The decriminalization efforts continued into the 1980s, but new legislative efforts advanced as well. In 1981, Congressman Stewart McKinney (R-Conn.) introduced H.R. 4498, "A bill to provide for the therapeutic use of marijuana in situations involving life-threatening illnesses and to provide adequate supplies of marijuana for such use." This groundbreaking proposal appears to be the first medical marijuana bill proposed in the U.S. Congress. Its support— it had eighty-four cosponsors, thirty-two Republicans and fifty-two Democrats—was even more notable. One of the first to cosponsor the bill was the future Speaker of the House Newt Gingrich (R-Ga.). Other cosponsors included future senators Judd Gregg (R-N.H.), Olympia Snowe (R-Me.), Tom Harkin (D-Iowa), and Jim Jeffords (R-Vt.).

The legislation was assertive. Its summary included an overview of the bill's main points:

- Amends the Controlled Substances Act to establish in the Department of Health and Human Services the Office for the Supply of Internationally Controlled Drugs, to be responsible for regulating the domestic production of marihuana and the distribution of marihuana for medical, scientific, and research purposes.

- Establishes procedures for the production of medicinal marihuana.
- Permits the distribution of medicinal marihuana only to hospitals and pharmacies registered to dispense Schedule II controlled substances for the purposes of treating glaucoma or the nausea of cancer patients or research approved under the Federal Food, Drug, and Cosmetic Act.

In many ways this legislation was ahead of its time, politically and medically. It was filed in the earliest of days of the AIDS epidemic, a disease that would later play a significant role in the medical marijuana movement and in 1987 take Congressman McKinney's life.

McKinney reintroduced the medical marijuana legislation in the Ninety-Eighth and Ninety-Ninth Congresses before dying early in the Hundredth Congress. Around that time, Ronald Reagan's War on Drugs was in full force and seemed to have a chilling effect on proposals for marijuana reform in Congress. In fact, there appears to have been no marijuana reform legislation proposed in the 100th, 101st, 102nd, and 103rd Congresses (1987–95). After Republicans took control of Congress in January 1995, marijuana reform legislation found new life.

On November 10, 1995, Congressman Barney Frank (D-Mass.) introduced H.R. 2618, "A bill to provide for the therapeutic use of marihuana in situations involving life-threatening or sense-threatening illnesses and to provide adequate supplies of marihuana for such use." In his floor speech introducing the legislation, Frank tipped his hat to his late colleague Stewart McKinney and noted the recent endorsement of medical marijuana by the American

Public Health Association, which he entered into the Congressional Record.[1] The legislation was multifaceted and comprehensive. It rescheduled marijuana to Schedule II. Similar to the McKinney legislation from the previous decade, it created the Office for the Supply of Internationally Controlled Drugs, charged with supplying medical marijuana to hospitals and pharmacies. It also defined qualifying conditions for medical treatment: nausea from cancer treatment, glaucoma, AIDS wasting syndrome, and spastic disorders of the muscles.

Frank's bill had eighteen cosponsors, including the future Speaker of the House Nancy Pelosi (D-Calif.), and a future senator and presidential candidate, Bernie Sanders (I-Vt.). Despite these sponsors it died in committee without being put to the vote.

The following Congress, gaveled in on January 3, 1997, turned out to be the setting for some of the most contentious marijuana policy infighting in congressional history. In response to California's legalizing medical marijuana, advocates on both sides of the issue ensured that the House and Senate would serve as arenas to voice their support or air their grievances about California's ballot measure.

In June 1997, Barney Frank reintroduced his medical marijuana legislation, but it also died in committee. Three other bills made clear Republicans' disdain for the California experiment. Senator Chuck Grassley of Iowa filed a resolution "expressing the sense of Congress in support of the existing Federal legal process for determining the safety and efficacy of drugs, including marijuana and other Schedule I drugs, for medicinal use" (S.J. Res. 57). Although the title of the bill conveyed scientific neutrality, the text of the bill declared, "Congress continues to support the existing Federal legal process for determining the safety and efficacy of drugs and opposes efforts to circumvent this process by legalizing marijuana . . . for medicinal use without valid scientific evidence."

Another resolution, introduced by Bill McCollum (R-Fla.), expressed "the sense of the House of Representatives that marijuana is a dangerous and addictive drug that should not be legalized for medical use" (H.Res. 372). McCollum had undergone a dramatic change of heart by the time he introduced this bill on September 16, 1998. Just sixteen years earlier, on March 1, 1982, McCollum, then a freshman congressman, had cosponsored, with Stewart McKinney, H.R. 4498, "A bill to provide for the therapeutic use of marijuana in situations involving life-threatening illnesses and to provide adequate supplies of marijuana for such use."[2]

The legislative bickering between the parties and between marijuana reformers and opponents would have no effect on federal law and amounted mostly to political grandstanding. Not until 2013 did Congress enact meaningful change in the area of marijuana policy. By then, several drug policy reform groups in Washington were in the process of implementing a decades-long strategy: professionalize and work within the system, Washington's governing framework. Marijuana Policy Project (MPP), Drug Policy Alliance (DPA), National Organization for the Reform of Marijuana Laws (NORML), Americans for Safe Access (ASA), and others looked more like D.C. power players than pot advocates. These groups had lobbyists, lawyers, communications pros, social media gurus, and growing clout. They understood the politics as well as the policy and began making progress toward legislative success.

With growing momentum from reform victories at the state and local levels and rapid change in public opinion, reform groups felt the wind at their back. They worked with reform-friendly legislators such as Earl Blumenauer (D-Ore.), Sam Farr (R-Calif.), Jared Polis (D-Colo.), Dana Rohrabacher (R-Calif.), and others to advance reform legislation.

In 2014, for the first time, a marijuana reform proposal gained majority support in Congress. On May 30 of that year, the House approved what was known as the Rohrabacher-Farr amendment by a 219–189 vote. The amendment, attached to the Department of Justice's funding bill, prohibited the DOJ from using funds "to prevent states from implementing their own state laws that authorize the use, distribution, possession or cultivation of medical marijuana."[3] That amendment was reauthorized in 2015 as part of FY2016 spending legislation.

Initially the effect of the legislation on policy was unclear. The DOJ argued the language in the bill did not restrict its power to prosecute individuals for marijuana violations under federal law. However, in *U.S. v. Marin Alliance for Medical Marijuana,* in 2015, a federal judge in the Northern District of California ordered the DOJ to comply with the law.

After Rohrabacher-Farr, the House and Senate separately began taking up marijuana legislation more frequently, dealing with banking issues for legal cannabis enterprises, extension of medical marijuana access for veterans living in states with legal systems, and protections for patients using cannabidiol oils. Each item passed only one chamber of Congress, but their majority support in even one chamber reflected the substantial progress made by marijuana reform advocacy groups. Just a decade earlier, marijuana reform legislation faced a certain fate: death in committee.

The success of the new professional-standard lobbying efforts extended beyond the majority votes in the House and Senate. The momentum was contagious. Members of Congress began proposing numerous bills seeking to address many aspects of the marijuana issue, including banking, taxation, rescheduling, veterans' access, children's access, criminal penalties, asset forfeiture, research, hemp cultivation, regulation, and more. Marijuana proposals extended to both medical and recreational marijuana. The new bills highlighted exactly how complex the issue is and how far the reform movement had advanced in convincing legislators that support for marijuana reform can be politically rewarding.

RESCHEDULING MARIJUANA Reform efforts at the federal level extended beyond Congress.[4] Some groups sought to lobby the executive branch with direct information campaigns and conversations among advocates, federal agencies, and the White House. Other efforts were more formal. One of the most visible and significant efforts to reform marijuana policy in the executive branch involved drug rescheduling.

What Is Drug Rescheduling?

Drug rescheduling means changing the schedule to which a drug has been assigned under the Controlled Substances

Act. There are five schedules; Schedule I drugs are deemed to be the most dangerous to both users and society as a whole, to have the highest "potential for abuse," and thus are subject to the highest level of control and sanctions. Congress made many of the initial determinations as to what drugs are in what schedule, but subsequent assignment or reassignment of drugs has been decided administratively. Since passage of the CSA, marijuana has been in Schedule I. As described in chapter 4, there are three criteria—the trifecta of prohibition—that lead to a substance being classified in Schedule I. One criterion is the substance has no medical value. The distinction also hampers research via a tremendous bureaucratic superstructure involving licensing, certification, security, background checks, and other requirements. It also creates cultural and societal biases against medical value and obstructs the scientific community from examining such value.

For all these reasons and more, many marijuana reformers want to get marijuana removed from Schedule I. The legal designations in the Controlled Substances Act and the substances that fall under them are not subject to regular review. Such review only occurs if the administration or an outside group initiates the process. That process is called rescheduling.

A common myth is that the president can use an executive order to reschedule marijuana. With a stroke of the pen—*poof!*—marijuana is no longer a Schedule I substance. Such an order would be in direct violation of federal law. Presidents cannot unilaterally reschedule marijuana, or any other substance. They can, however, play a significant role in the process, as the details of rescheduling procedure make clear.

Rescheduling can happen in two ways. The first way is that Congress can amend the CSA to make changes. Such an amendment can include the movement of a substance from one schedule to another, or off of the schedules entirely. The second way is through administrative action, as provided in section 201 of the CSA.

How Rescheduling Actually Works

Administrative rescheduling—a long, arduous, and complex process involving numerous actors—is spelled out quite precisely in the CSA statute. The process starts in the Office of the Attorney General. The attorney general or another official such as the secretary of Health and Human Services (HHS) can initiate a review, or an outside group can file a petition requesting a substance be rescheduled.

The attorney general reviews the petition and also submits it to the secretary of Health and Human Services for review. By custom that review is delegated to the FDA (this is not specified in the wording of the CSA). The CSA, in Section 201(2)(b), does specify that the review must include "a scientific and medical evaluation, and his [secretary of HHS] recommendations as to whether such drug or other substance should be so controlled or removed as a controlled substance" and must consider five factors about the substance:

1. Scientific evidence of its pharmacological effect, if known . . .
2. The state of current scientific knowledge regarding the drug or other substance . . .
3. What, if any, risk there is to public health . . .
4. Its psychic or physiological dependence liability . . .

6. Whether the substance is an immediate precursor of a substance already controlled

The review must also consider "any scientific or medical considerations" involving "its actual or relative potential for abuse . . . its history and current pattern of abuse . . . [and] the scope, duration, and significance of abuse."[5] Once the report is complete, the FDA transmits it to the secretary of HHS, who then sends the findings and recommendation to the attorney general.

Simultaneous with the FDA review, the attorney general also reviews the petition according to the same criteria but typically delegates the task to the DEA. If the HHS secretary recommends that a drug *not* be controlled—that it be descheduled—that finding "shall be binding on the Attorney General."[6] Otherwise, the attorney general is charged with compiling the evidence, reviewing it, and issuing an order about whether to maintain a drug's current schedule or to reschedule it.

That may sound like it is the end of the road, but statutorily it is not. In practice, the greatest hurdles are still ahead. If the attorney general determines that a drug should be rescheduled, that order initiates the so-called rulemaking process—which can also be lengthy, confusing, and complex—before a final rule—a regulation—is issued.[7] Although the CSA appears to empower the attorney general in significant ways, she is not the only official likely to influence the rescheduling process.

Drug policy in the United States affects a wide variety of public policies—criminal justice, taxes, medicine and science, law enforcement, commerce, banking, trade, and so forth. An attorney general's determination regarding the rescheduling of a substance must reflect consideration of all of those aspects and interests, and one would also expect that given the historical contentiousness of this issue, there would be input and influence from the White House. In addition, if a drug is to be rescheduled, the rule-making process is initiated, and if the proposed rule (regulation) is deemed "economically significant," the Office of Information and Regulatory Affairs within the White House's Office of Management and Budget must conduct a review of the rule. A marijuana rescheduling rule could certainly be deemed economically significant and would trigger a formal (in addition to the informal) involvement of the White House.

Once that rule is finalized, once the petition has cleared all of the hurdles—thresholds, decisionmakers, and agency analyses—the substance is rescheduled.

A Brief History of Marijuana Rescheduling Petitions
As of 2016, four petitions had been filed to reschedule marijuana.[8] The first came in 1972, when the National Organization for the Reform of Marijuana Laws (NORML) used the language of the statute to first test the attorney general's willingness to reconsider marijuana's Schedule I status. This was groundbreaking and pioneering work in the area of marijuana reform, and the Justice Department was likely caught off guard. Initially, the DOJ and the DEA opted not to review the petition, forcing NORML to sue in federal court in an effort to force the agency to meet its duty under the CSA. The U.S. Court of Appeals issued rulings in 1974, 1977, and 1980 ordering that the petition be reviewed. The DEA failed to comply, necessitating

repeated suits and rulings. During this fight the DEA's administrative law judge even ruled, famously, that the DEA should reschedule marijuana, but the agency rejected both the judge's recommendation and the petition. The petition was formally denied in 1989.

The second rescheduling petition was filed in 1995 by the marijuana reform activist Jon Gettman and *High Times* magazine.[9] This petition also stalled within the DEA for years. During that time the White House's Office of National Drug Control Policy commissioned the Institute of Medicine (IOM), a division of the National Academies of Science, Engineering and Medicine, to study the question of marijuana's suitability as a Schedule I substance and issue a report. Published in 1999, the report "summarizes and analyzes what is known about the medical use of marijuana; it emphasizes evidence-based medicine."[10] Its findings aligned with and thus provided tacit support for Gettman's petition, explaining: "The accumulated data indicate a potential therapeutic value for cannabinoid drugs, particularly for symptoms such as pain relief, control of nausea and vomiting, and appetite stimulation. The therapeutic effects of cannabinoids are best established for THC, which is generally one of the two most abundant of the cannabinoids in marijuana. . . . It is important to point out that Schedule I status does not necessarily apply to all cannabinoids."[11]

The IOM report called for additional research into cannabinoids and the therapeutic effects of certain cannabinoids, under certain conditions, for the treatment of specific ailments. Such a report should have influenced the government that both commissioned the report and was charged with reconsidering marijuana's Schedule I status, but it did not. Two years after the release of the report, the Justice Department rejected Gettman's petition.

In 2002, Gettman filed the third marijuana rescheduling petition, this time with a group of medical marijuana patients who were living evidence of the therapeutic benefits of marijuana in the treatment of illnesses. In 2011 this petition, too, was denied. The government argued that there was insufficient research into the efficacy of marijuana for medical use, its potential for abuse, or its safe use in treatment. It was a perfect catch-22: the widely recognized reality is that marijuana's Schedule I status is what restricts the type of research needed to evaluate whether marijuana should remain in Schedule I.[12]

The fourth petition seeking to reschedule marijuana was filed in 2011 by elected officials. Then Governors Christine Gregoire (D-Wash.) and Lincoln Chafee (I-R.I.) submitted the petition as governors of states with medical marijuana programs with the aim of achieving needed legal clarity. The DEA typically provides no status or progress updates on their review; however, in spring 2016, in response to an information request from the United States Senate, the DEA noted it was expecting to make a determination on the rescheduling petition by summer 2016.

ELEVEN THE FIGHT FOR MEDICAL MARIJUANA

MARIJUANA HAS BEEN USED in the treatment of a variety of ailments for millennia, and that practice continues today in many U.S. states and in nations throughout the world. However, marijuana was effectively banned in the United States in the 1930s, and in 1970 Congress formally declared marijuana to have no medical value and made its medical use formally illegal. Many early reform efforts focused on decriminalization (discussed in chapter 9), a criminal justice reform that was silent on medicinal value. Rescheduling efforts since the 1970s have focused on marijuana's medicinal value, but so far have been unsuccessful.

As Americans continue to use marijuana for relief from a variety of medical conditions, states and even the federal government have taken steps to relax or eliminate absolute prohibition. The path to that point, however, was a long, bitter, and brutal fight involving a social movement born in the Bay Area over a decade before California formally approved medical marijuana.

DENNIS PERON'S CAMPAIGN OF COMPASSION IN CALIFORNIA

That effort began in San Francisco in the late 1980s. In his award-winning book, *Weed the People*, Bruce Barcott eloquently writes of the role the AIDS epidemic played in reviving and growing the medical marijuana movement. Many people were involved in early medical marijuana reform efforts. Parallel movements worked together and sometimes in competition with one another. Several leaders emerged on this issue, but in those early days, one man stood out: Dennis Peron.

Peron is a businessman, an activist, a community organizer, and a proud gay American. He lived in a community in San Francisco that was ravaged by the AIDS epidemic, particularly in the late 1980s and early 1990s. He watched friends, neighbors, and even his partner waste away from the disease. As AIDS enters its final stages the symptoms are horrifying. The cocktails of life-sustaining (or really death-delaying) medicines that were available in the 1980s and 1990s came with terrible side effects.

Peron's partner and other friends suffering from the disease found some relief from using marijuana. Cannabis wasn't a cure, but it helped—helped people who felt helpless. For Peron, the issue became a crusade—a drug war of his own. He organized his community, disseminated information, and worked with government officials first in San Francisco and eventually in Sacramento. He engaged dedicated activists and others who did what they could to help—people such as Mary Rathbun, a volunteer in San Francisco General Hospital's AIDS unit who baked brownies laced with marijuana and, on her rounds, delivered them to dying AIDS patients. She came to be called "Brownie Mary."

Peron, along with members of the community, investors, and friends like Brownie Mary, eventually started the Cannabis Buyers Club in the Castro neighborhood of San Francisco. During the 1990s this illegal dispensary delivered cannabis to many sick patients—not just AIDS patients. Peron and his associates faced harassment from police, raids, multiple arrests, and asset seizures. Despite those hurdles, Peron continued his mission as soon as he was freed from lockup. He eventually translated that energy into a political cause: to get Proposition 215 (known formally as the Compassionate Use Act of 1996), to legalize access to medical marijuana, on the 1996 ballot in California.

Peron's passion sometimes worked against him, leading him to step on toes, alienate even allies, and put the entire movement to pass Proposition 215 into jeopardy. Working at times with Peron and at times in spite of him, a group of outside, professional, well-funded organizers came to the eleventh-hour rescue in California when the effort to gather the half million signatures needed to qualify for the ballot seemed to be faltering. Ethan Nadelmann (later the founder of the Drug Policy Alliance) and others stepped in to push the signature drive over the finish line.[1] Proposition 215 went before California voters on November 5, 1996, and passed with 55.6 percent of the votes. In all, it would receive 5,382,915 votes—260,000 more votes than President Bill Clinton would receive from Californians that night as he was reelected.

THE FEDERAL RESPONSE   The passage of Proposition 215 created a legal puzzle. The state of California declared that medical marijuana was legal, that patients had a right to access it, and that it could be grown to supply those patients. But the Controlled Substances Act explicitly outlawed what California said was legal. In the eyes of federal authorities, the California proposition was meaningless: it did nothing to change federal law, and federal law is supreme.

But the situation put the Clinton administration in a bind. Clinton was the first president to admit having tried marijuana; he also came to the White House on the heels of a twelve-year intensification of the drug war under the Reagan and Bush administrations. He could not look soft on crime. Being soft on marijuana would also fly in the face of Clinton's message to American youth: "Drugs are wrong, drugs are illegal, and drugs can kill you."[2] Yet, California is a big place and federal law enforcement was too small a force to arrest everyone violating the CSA under the umbrella of the Compassionate Use Act. If a federal response to Proposition 215 failed, Clinton would also look weak and ineffective.

Federal officials also had other concerns. Although the Compassionate Use Act was about delivering medical cannabis to the elderly, the ill, and the dying, the administration worried that California's medical marijuana system would end up serving as an opening for the legalization of recreational marijuana. The architecture of Prop 215 did little to assuage those concerns, as the system was largely unregulated.

Those fears were compounded as more states legalized medical marijuana without strict regulatory systems or market controls in place. Oregon, Washington, and Colorado joined California in "the wild west of weed." There is no doubt these early distribution systems provided cannabis to sick individuals desperate for relief from their symptoms. There is also no doubt that for many, the early, unregulated medical marijuana systems functioned as proxy markets for recreational users seeking legal weed. In fact, it would be years before these states passed reforms to effectively regulate their medical marijuana distribution systems.

In the meantime, the Clinton and George W. Bush administrations tried to enforce federal law, authorizing the DEA and the FBI to work with local law enforcement to raid medical marijuana operations across the American West. Grow operations and processors were shut down. Co-op participants were handcuffed and assets were seized. Anecdotes abound of terminally ill patients being treated like street criminals for being caught tending their plants when federal agents arrived.

These Clinton- and especially Bush-era SWAT-style raids revealed three important things about medical marijuana. First, marijuana was (and still is) illegal under federal law in all jurisdictions. Federal officials had (and in some cases still have) the power and legal authority to intervene in marijuana grow operations. State-level legalization of medical marijuana has become a significant locus of dramatic federal-state tension.

Second, these raids also showed the limits to federal enforcement power. Despite hundreds of raids in the late 1990s and 2000s, medical marijuana growers and systems continued to flourish. Farms and co-ops were closed and dispensaries shuttered, but new ones popped up almost immediately. Sometimes new grows rose like phoenixes from the ashes of the same plots of land that had been raided by federal agents just days or weeks before.

Third, these raids showed that every push by the feds caused a pull in the opposite direction by activists. Federal intervention did not scare medical marijuana operators into compliance and submission. In fact, government-sponsored fear campaigns basically ran into a brick wall in California. The activist community, growers, patients, customers, and even some local officials responded with renewed energy to advance their cause. And that energy was contagious. Even in the face of fierce government efforts to stop medical marijuana, other states were not intimidated; they were inspired to set up systems of their own. By almost any metric the enforcement-by-raid approach of the 1990s and 2000s failed.

When widespread raids failed to solve the administrations' problems, another solution was crafted by the ONDCP and the Clinton-era drug czar, a former general, Barry McCaffrey. Under Prop 215, patients could only access medical marijuana if a board-certified physician gave them a recommendation. A recommendation became the manner in which doctors gave patients access to medical marijuana, as it is illegal to use a DEA-regulated prescription pad to authorize use of an illegal substance. Effectively, a recommendation is a doctor's note saying the person has a medical condition that marijuana can help treat. "The drug czar pegged physicians as the weakest link in the med-pot chain," writes Martin Lee of McCaffrey's brainstorm. "Cut them out of the picture and there would be no way for folks to secure the requisite recommendation."[3] To that end, McCaffrey put out a warning to doctors: "A practitioner's action of recommending or prescribing Schedule I controlled substances is not consistent with the 'public interest' . . . and will lead to administrative action by the Drug Enforcement Administration to revoke the practitioner's registration."[4]

In effect, McCaffrey threatened doctors that if they recommended marijuana to a patient, they would lose their legal right to issue prescriptions entirely—a career killer for any physician. In addition to the doctor-targeted threat, the Clinton administration continued the raids on grow operations, caretaker facilities, and other cannabis enterprises and arrests of growers and even sick patients. The president who tried to puff pot as a Rhodes Scholar showed no sign of sympathy in waging the War on Drugs in California.

The White House and ONDCP policy of strategically targeting doctors in an effort to destroy California's medical marijuana program eventually came to an end. A group of doctors, patients, and advocacy organizations sued over the policy. *Conant v. McCaffrey* was decided in 2002 by the U.S. Court of Appeals for the Ninth Circuit.[5] In the ruling, the court noted that the government could not initiate administrative or criminal proceedings against a doctor simply for recommending marijuana. The case was a win for doctors and patients and presented a challenge for the government's effort to stop state medical marijuana programs, and the U.S. Supreme Court allowed the ruling to stand by refusing to hear the case.

MEDICAL MARIJUANA THRIVES   Unlike the history of marijuana decriminalization, which went through active and dormant periods, medical marijuana grew like a weed. Just two years after Prop 215 passed, Alaska, Oregon, and Washington followed suit. The floodgates were open, and soon numerous states joined the original pathbreakers: Maine (1999); Colorado, Hawaii, and Nevada (2000); Montana and Vermont (2004); Rhode Island (2006); New Mexico (2007); Michigan (2008); Arizona, the District of Columbia, and New Jersey (2010); Delaware (2011); Connecticut and Massachusetts (2012); New York and Illinois (2013); Maryland, Minnesota, and New York (2014); Pennsylvania and Ohio (2016). By the start of 2016, twenty-five states and the District of Columbia had established or were in the process of establishing medical marijuana programs.

By the start of 2016, sixteen other states had passed laws allowing the medical use of cannabidiol oils (illegal under the CSA).[6] Earlier efforts to reform laws in these states had often focused on children with epilepsy and the relief some find using this nonpsychoactive cannabis extract. However, most of the programs were quite limited and failed to provide a market or a means for parents, families, and patients to procure the oil legally. In fact, most states provided patients and their families an "affirmative defense": although they could be arrested, booked, and tried for possession of CBD, the law gave them the right to use their medical condition, recommendation from a doctor, and existing state law as a defense against conviction. It was very small-scale reform, but for the parents of children with intractable epilepsy, many were willing to take anything they could get.

The variety of medical marijuana programs in the United States showed the laboratories of democracy at work. To be sure, problems existed in early systems. The California system, for example, was often criticized for being a loose program that doubled as a proxy for a recreational system. That criticism emerged because of meager regulations in a variety of areas that were reinforced by courts when the legislature tried to amend the system. Others, like Colorado's initial medical marijuana experiment, were often derided as the "Wild West"; the saying went that there were more marijuana dispensaries than Starbucks in Denver.

With each additional system, lessons have been learned and processes improved. No two state systems are identical. The creation, design, and execution of state medical marijuana programs has involved some level of political compromise, and local interests and issues have affected what a program ultimately looks like, regardless of initial intentions. Under some systems, patients can grow their own or delegate their grow operation to a (usually small) coop or consortium run by an individual, called a caretaker, who then provides the patient her share of marijuana. Other states developed robust commercial markets that function like a liquor store or a pastry shop. Some states set forth a very limited number of qualifying conditions (diagnoses that meet program eligibility). Still other states gave doctors broad discretion to identify the medical need for marijuana, regardless of the condition. States instituted a range of regulatory demands—some quite strict, others less so. Some states opted to treat marijuana like alcohol, others like a pharmaceutical; still others treat it unlike any other product or service. Oversight of programs also varies, ranging from alcohol control boards to tax collection agencies to departments of health to departments of consumer protection and more.

The variation in state systems illustrates a few points. First, there is no one-size-fits-all model for a state medical marijuana program. Second, there is no effective, centralized clearinghouse of best practices that well inform states that are launching programs. Often, state leaders and regulators tour other states' systems to gather information they can use in designing their own system, but despite efforts from marijuana advocacy organizations and groups like the National Conference of State Legislatures, attempts to comprehensively identify best practices have not come fully to fruition. Third, despite ongoing federal government enforcement and busts, the systems are broadly functional, even in the face of federal prohibition. Fourth, regulatory decisions are not one-shot deals. Multiple states have revised their rules, regulations, or even entire regulatory structures. California, Colorado, Montana, and Washington, for example, have learned from their initial mistakes and have taken steps to improve their original medical marijuana programs.

ONGOING BATTLES IN THE WAR
FOR MEDICAL MARIJUANA REFORM   For the advocacy community the fight over medical marijuana does not end when

a state approves a program but rather continues on many fronts. In 2005, the U.S. Supreme Court ruled in *Gonzales v. Raich* that the federal government could still enforce the law against marijuana users, growers, and enterprises, even in states that have reformed laws to allow use, production, and distribution. That ruling perpetuates the existence of the legal gray area in which medical marijuana systems operate. Raids continue (some of them targeting genuine "bad actors" even under state law), and those arrested cannot use a state's medical marijuana laws as an affirmative defense in federal court. Even in the face of state-level successes, advocacy organizations continue to seek further, more comprehensive reform.

One such reform, focused on issues at the federal level, was the 2015 Compassionate Access, Research Expansion, and Respect States Act. As briefly mentioned in chapter 8, the goal of CARERS was to achieve six changes that would eliminate the legal gray area surrounding the federal-state disconnect on medical marijuana: (1) Let states set up medical marijuana programs and exempt people from federal punishment if they comply with state law. (2) Reschedule marijuana to Schedule II. (3) Deschedule cannabidiol. (4) End the DEA-mandated, NIDA-enforced monopoly for growing research-grade marijuana (currently grown exclusively at the University of Mississippi). (5) Let Veterans Administration doctors in medical marijuana states recommend marijuana to their patients. (6) Give cannabis enterprises access to banking services.

As of mid-2016, no action had been taken on the CARERS Act, the most serious proposal yet to deal with the inconsistencies in federal marijuana law and policy. Those inconsistencies continue and, with each new state reform, increase. Ongoing legal challenges and the changing conversation around marijuana policy at the federal and state levels have driven additional congressional support for passage of CARERS. In the Senate, 2016 brought additional support, including some ideologically opposed senators like Lindsey Graham (R-S.C.) and Chris Murphy (D-Conn.). The House companion bill was dormant until October 2015, but between October 2015 and April 2016, the number of CARERS Act cosponsors more than doubled, from sixteen to thirty-six, suggesting that minds are changing and momentum is growing to pass the bill.

Because of reformers' unrelenting efforts, in 2016, over 160 million Americans lived in states with medical marijuana programs, and were able to get treatment for symptoms of such ailments as AIDS wasting syndrome, chemotherapy side effects, multiple sclerosis, anxiety, chronic pain, epilepsy, and many others. In spite of Congress's declaration that marijuana has no medical value and cannot be safely used in medical treatment, hundreds of thousands of Americans now use that drug safely every day.

TWELVE RECREATIONAL MARIJUANA SPROUTS IN THE WEST

IN NOVEMBER 2012, America started legalizing recreational marijuana for adult use. Starting with Colorado and Washington and followed by Alaska, Oregon, and the District of Columbia just two years later, these states passed ballot initiatives to embrace the most extensive marijuana policy reforms to date.

The movement to legalize marijuana for recreational use focused on parallels with adults making choices about the use of an intoxicating substance that they would access through a regulated system—namely, alcohol. Advocates of marijuana legalization point to the failures of alcohol prohibition to argue that a regulated adult-use market proved a better alternative for alcohol and the same would be true for marijuana. Post-legalization most state-level marijuana regulation occurs in the same institutions that regulate alcohol. That regulatory choice is not surprising given that alcohol regulators deal with an intoxicating substance, available in a variety of forms with varying levels of potency, that is only accessible to adults twenty-one and over in strictly structured sales settings.

As with battles over alcohol prohibition and legalization, the fight to legalize adult-use marijuana has a long and storied history. Understanding why and how this movement progressed to the eventual passage of full-scale legalization offers insight into the future of the movement.

WHY LEGALIZATION? Legalization of recreational marijuana isn't universally supported, but in four states and the District of Columbia, a majority of voters have decided it is an acceptable policy for them. The reasons why people voted to approve these ballot initiatives vary widely. This is an aspect of legalization reform that is often lost in media coverage. The choice to legalize is not an on/off switch by which votes just decide yes or no. Voters also think about "why?" So, it's important to review some of the reasons people support full legalization. Not surprisingly, many people's vote reflects some combination of factors.

RIGHTS AND FREEDOM. One basic argument in favor of legalization is a libertarian one: Individuals should have the right to make choices about the substances they use. Marijuana is no more (and is likely less) harmful than alcohol and tobacco, and if the government lets adults make choices about those substances, they should get out of the way of people making that choice about cannabis. Given the prevalence of libertarian values in the American West, it is likely that this argument carried some weight in the first four states to legalize recreational marijuana.

RACIAL JUSTICE. Racial disparities exist in the criminal justice system in the United States, and these disparities are particularly obvious in cases involving marijuana. Many people recognize that legalization can help limit those disparities and the consequences of marijuana arrests for communities of color. According to a comprehensive 2013 report from the American Civil Liberties Union, black arrest rates for marijuana possession far outpace white arrest rates, even though marijuana use is about the same between both groups. Despite being 15 percent of the national population, blacks accounted for 58 percent of marijuana arrests in 2010.[1] Those disparities are affecting a significant number of Americans. The ACLU report notes that between 2001 and 2010, there were 7 million marijuana arrests, of which 88 percent were for possession, and during that time the disparities in arrest rates between blacks and whites increased significantly. In fact, in a case study of New York City, researchers found not only were there racial disparities in marijuana arrests, but those disparities extended to punishment and sentencing.[2] People of all races resent that type of unequal treatment, and many see legalization as a step in the right direction.

THE HEAVY COSTS OF PROHIBITION. Dollars and cents also motivate voters to support marijuana legalization. Tremendous sums of money are spent on enforcing federal and state marijuana laws every year. A 2010 study by

Harvard economist Jeffrey Miron puts that total cost at around $14 billion annually for federal and local law enforcement, judicial, and corrections costs. Many voters believe that because marijuana arrests are so heavily skewed toward simple possession, legalization would mean cost savings and ultimately smarter budgeting. Those funds, some voters argue, could be better spent in other law enforcement capacities, on drug treatment, or in other areas entirely. As the 2012 legalization initiatives began to get organized, the United States was still recovering from a major recession, and state and local budgets had been slashed. Those budget realities put into focus the importance of making hard choices. For some, that conversation made marijuana legalization an easy choice.

TAX REVENUE. The tax revenue argument begins with the awareness that marijuana is used throughout society and that individuals purchase from the illegal market every day. Those transactions are outside the government purview and thus cannot be taxed. Prohibition of marijuana represents a lost revenue opportunity. One of the selling points of marijuana legalization is that, if legal, the product can generate tax revenue. Marijuana-legal states use the additional revenue to help balance budgets and pay for regulatory and enforcement activities required by the system. By legalizing marijuana and transitioning customers from the illegal to the legal, the government can reap the benefits of an existing market.

ECONOMIC BENEFITS. The illegal market creates jobs and gives people an income. The legal market does that, and more: it spurs innovation, provides employment for additional staff of many kinds, and supports dynamic secondary and tertiary markets such as construction, security, agricultural products, and food preparation, among others. The legalization of marijuana can pump money into the economy, create jobs directly in the industry and beyond, and offer people a safer, more secure employment opportunity than the black market. This is a large and growing economic sector. From January to November 2015, about $900 million worth of medical and recreational marijuana was sold in Colorado alone, and the December totals were expected to push the figure past the $1 billion mark.[3] Those benefits simply involve direct spending, and exclude any effects on secondary markets or the impact of marijuana tourism, which has been shown to be significant. Pot pumps money into a state economy and legal pot has an even larger effect.

DISPLACEMENT OF ILLEGAL MARKETS. Some want legalized marijuana in an effort to put black market drug dealers and their suppliers out of business. Concerns abound about the crime associated with illegal markets—of all kinds—and in the context of drugs, many worry about the power and influx of cartel activity into communities. One goal of legalization is to buffer states from the impact and consequences of the illicit drug market. Some early evidence suggests that legalization in Colorado is having such intended effects.[4]

REGULATION AND PRODUCT SAFETY. Product safety is another benefit of the legal market. The argument here is: if people are going to buy marijuana, regardless of its legal status, they ought to know what they are getting. Buyers purchasing marijuana on the illegal market are often uncertain about the quality, safety, composition, and potency of the product. Strict regulatory schemes for grow environments, product testing, titration, and sampling help ensure that consumers knows just what they are getting and can be confident that the marijuana was grown in a safe environment.

MEETING CONSUMER DEMAND. Perhaps the most obvious reason for supporting marijuana legalization—one that is often overlooked in the debate—is that some people just like smoking pot. Quite apart from the many ethical and economic reasons for supporting legal adult use, people demand it. People like it, just as they like having a drink or a cigarette or a cigar. For some people this is likely the primary reason for supporting legalization.

HOW LEGALIZATION HAPPENED

Advocacy on behalf of marijuana legalization at the grassroots level has been around for some time, but not until 2012 was an initiative successful. Part of the momentum toward legalization grew out of changes in public opinion on the issue nationally and in the states (see chapter 7). And a major factor behind legalization's success was the continued professionalization of the movement.

I just enumerated some of the very good reasons for people to support legalization. But translating those desires and opinions into an effective campaign to pass marijuana legalization is no easy task and is not one that amateurs can mount successfully on a statewide scale. The movement had to bring in professional help. For a statewide initiative, success requires three important elements (other than funding): issue expertise, general political skill, and an in-depth knowledge of a place and its people. Much of that support came from a cadre of lawyers, fundraisers, communications specialists, pollsters, strategists, and others who brought to the table a unique blend of skills that gave legalization a chance. This brain trust of the marijuana movement included dozens of high-profile, longtime legalization supporters, including two Denver-area attorneys, Brian Vicente and Christian Sederberg; Steve Fox, Ethan Nadelmann, and Rob Kampia, heads of national marijuana advocacy organizations; Alison Holcomb of the ACLU; Pete Holmes, the city attorney of Seattle; Graham Boyd, an attorney and adviser to the late Peter Lewis; and Mason Tvert, a communications professional and field organizer. And many, many others.

This group applied their own political, policy, and strategic expertise to focus on a communications strategy, fundraising, advertising, get-out-the-vote initiatives, and message testing and targeting. The latter activities were among the most important. The groups working in Colorado and Washington learned from past successful and unsuccessful ballot initiatives for medical and recreational marijuana. They understood that crafting an effective message or set of messages and delivering those messages to the right groups of people at the right times was absolutely essential for success. In addition, packaging that messaging in a way that connected with the specific groups was a must. In the process, the teams understood the diversity of views held, not just on whether to legalize marijuana, but on why, and those considerations informed the design of the campaigns.

Any campaign requires coalition building and ensuring that the language of the initiative matches the demands, expectations, ideologies, demographics, and political realities of a given state at a given time. That process begins with an understanding of what the different demographic groups in a state need, want, or must be convinced of, and then crafting an initiative that reflects those considerations. Campaigns that do this effectively are successful. Those that don't, fail, as happened in Ohio's 2015 legalization initiative.

Crafting the language of a marijuana legalization ballot initiative is not simple—it is not an easy yes or no. The wording of the ballot question must reflect a detailed and nuanced set of choices. These initiatives succeed or fail depending on how they handle issues like homegrow rights, local autonomy and opt-out provisions, market structure, jurisdiction of regulation, the scope of regulatory power, tax policy, protections for existing medical marijuana systems, combatting addiction, protecting children, and lowering crime.

What do those choices show? Marijuana legalization is complex, mainstream public policy that has as much to do with good and effective governance as it does with providing legal access to cannabis. So far, in four states and the District of Columbia, the drafters of the initiatives got the language right, and the organizers found the right messaging and strategy to build a successful coalition.

Colorado, 2012: Amendment 64
On November 6, 2012, with the support of 55 percent of voters, Colorado approved Amendment 64, a constitutional amendment allowing recreational marijuana in the

state. The amendment itself, subsequent legislation, and regulations combined to create the nation's first system to get off the ground. Marijuana sales from dispensaries began on January 1, 2014. Under the system, any individual twenty-one years and older can purchase marijuana from a state-licensed and -regulated dispensary. Colorado residents can purchase one ounce at a time, and out-of-state residents can purchase one-quarter ounce.

The system functions as a heavily regulated private market in which growers, processors, and dispensaries are private enterprises. Initially the system was vertically integrated, meaning that dispensary owners also had to grow and process at least 80 percent of the marijuana they sold. By the following year, the vertical integration requirement had expired in most parts of the state. In addition, initial licenses to operate in the recreational market were open only to existing medical marijuana enterprises. That requirement also included a sunset provision.

The state implemented a seed-to-sale electronic tracking system, as well as extensive security requirements for marijuana facilities in an effort to prevent theft or loss ("diversion"). The state levies substantial taxes on marijuana transactions at the price point, including a 15 percent special marijuana tax, a 10 percent marijuana sales tax (to be reduced to 8 percent in July 2017), the standard 2.9 percent state sales tax, and any additional county or municipal taxes or fees. Tax collection as well as the regulatory jurisdiction for the recreational and medical marijuana programs rest with the Department of Revenue's Marijuana Enforcement Division.[5]

In addition, Amendment 64 gives Coloradans a constitutional right to have a homegrow, a system under which

Colorado residents can grow up to six marijuana plants, of which three can be flowering at a given time. This alternative to the commercial market is allowed so long as residents comply with all state laws and local zoning laws regarding grows. A local government can opt out of the commercial market, banning private marijuana enterprises from setting up shop, but it cannot ban an individual property owner from growing marijuana. In addition, the amendment bans public use of marijuana, and the state's Indoor Clean Air Act is used as justification to ban use in businesses or other facilities. Finally, the amendment gives the state legislature and the Department of Revenue fairly broad discretion to create and modify regulations to ensure the success of the program. But since the reform was the result of a constitutional amendment, some policies are fixed and can be revised only by means of a subsequent amendment.

Washington State, 2012: Initiative 502

On November 6, 2012, voters in Washington joined Coloradans in approving recreational marijuana. Initiative 502 was approved with 56 percent of the vote. Whereas Colorado voted on an amendment to its constitution, the initiative created a set of new state statutes, which can be amended by a vote of the state legislature (or by another initiative). Sales of marijuana began in July 2014, making pot available to customers twenty-one and older, who can purchase up to one ounce of marijuana from a state-licensed and -regulated dispensary.

As in Colorado, the market is private and heavily regulated. The regulatory body is the Liquor and Cannabis Board (the Liquor Control Board until July 2015). The market bans vertical integration, meaning dispensary owners cannot grow the product they sell nor process it. The one exception to the vertical integration rule is that growers and processors can combine into one entity.

Initially, taxation was a tiered system of excise taxes. The grower, processor, and dispensary were each required to pay a 25 percent tax on product transfers and sales. The exception was that if a grower and processor combined to a joint venture, that entity would only have to pay a 25 percent tax on the transfer to a dispensary, dramatically lowering the tax burden. For a variety of reasons, including business tax and expense reporting, the Washington legislature amended the marijuana taxation provisions. Starting in mid-2015, marijuana was taxed with a flat 37 percent state excise tax. Customers were also required to pay any additional local taxes.

Initiative 502 was silent on localities' ability to opt out of the new recreational marijuana program, but several municipalities have used zoning laws to implement de facto opt-outs by banning commercial cannabis operations in that jurisdiction. The opt-out option is similar to Colorado's, but in Washington, it introduces an additional challenge to the consumer because Washington has banned homegrows, so Washingtonians who live in an opt-out location and desire legal marijuana must drive to a municipality in which dispensaries are allowed to operate in order to purchase. The initiative also bans public use of marijuana, cannabis clubs, and use in other establishments. The legislature has substantial authority to amend the provisions of the initiative because the reform is statutory, and even within the existing provisions of the initiative, the legislature and regulatory bodies have substantial authority to create and maintain the details of the program at their discretion.

Alaska, 2014: Ballot Measure 2

Alaska joined the ranks of states legalizing recreational marijuana on November 4, 2014, when 52 percent of voters approved Ballot Measure 2, creating a set of state statutes allowing marijuana to be grown, processed, and sold in the Land of the Midnight Sun. The state intended to begin issuing licenses to producers in mid-2016, delaying the start of legal sales likely into 2017. When sales begin, state-licensed and -regulated dispensaries will be authorized to dispense up to one ounce of marijuana to customers twenty-one and over.

As in other states, Alaska's marijuana program is a private and heavily regulated system. The program's regulatory authority rests with the Alcohol and Marijuana Control Office (until 2016 the Alcohol Beverage Control Board) in the Alaska Department of Commerce. Within the office, a five-member Marijuana Control Board maintains substantial authority over the system and the market dynamics. In Alaska, vertical integration is allowed (unlike in Washington), but it is not required (as it initially was in Colorado). Cannabis enterprises can choose to operate in one, some, or all parts of the supply chain.

By the start of 2016, the rules surrounding taxation were still being proposed. The ballot measure offered a starting point for taxation ($50 per ounce transferred from the grower), but allowed the Alaska Department of Revenue to modify that rate. Ultimately, the Department of Revenue proposed a tax of $50 per ounce of whole flower and $15 per ounce of trim. In addition, municipalities are able to enact a local sales tax on transactions.

Alaska allows municipalities to opt out of the legal marijuana program if they desire. However, Alaska has a complicated municipal system in which huge swaths of the state are unincorporated villages to which the title "municipality" doesn't apply. So, the state legislature and regulatory bodies are working to design a policy that deals with villages' local choices. Alaska does, however, allow homegrows—a tradition that dates back to a 1975 Alaska Supreme Court decision that extended privacy rights on one's property to marijuana production.

The Alaska model does not allow the public use of marijuana, but the state pioneered a scenario whereby the Marijuana Control Board issued regulations that would allow cannabis clubs, or the consumption of marijuana on-site at dispensaries under strict conditions. Such a policy was the first such effort in the United States. Under Ballot Measure 2 the legislature has substantial authority to make subsequent changes to the law, except that the legislature may not overturn a ballot measure within two years of passage. Otherwise, the measure offers the legislature, the Alcohol and Marijuana Control Office, and, to a lesser extent, the Department of Revenue, substantial discretion over administering the state's marijuana program.

Oregon, 2014: Measure 91
On November 4, 2014, Oregon also voted to legalize recreational marijuana. This move was historically fitting. In 1973, Oregon became the first state to decriminalize marijuana and, in 1998, the second state to approve a

medical marijuana program. It joined Alaska and the District of Columbia as part of the second wave of legalization just two years after Colorado and Washington had led the way. The measure received support from 56 percent of voters and, as in Alaska and Washington, created a statutory authorization for recreational marijuana. Limited recreational sales began in October 2015; the limited system is projected to be in place until January 2017. Until the state issues licenses for the recreational market and that market becomes productive, customers twenty-one and older can purchase up to one-quarter ounce, as available, from some medical marijuana dispensaries in the state.

Once the system is up and running it will be similar to that in other states: a private, heavily regulated market. Measure 91 gave the Oregon Liquor Control Commission regulatory jurisdiction over the system. The market, once licensed and functional, can be vertically integrated, but it is not a requirement. In this respect, the model is one of businesses' choice, as in Alaska.

Measure 91 initially devised a tax system based on product weight, rather than price point. However, that tax model was replaced through a legislative effort (H.B. 2041). That legislation instituted taxes at the point of sale, like a standard sales tax. The tax rate would range from 17 to 20 percent, given a base tax rate of 17 percent and municipal government's option to institute an additional tax up to 3 percent. That tax would apply once the recreational system became operational. During the interim period, while limited recreational sales were made via medical marijuana dispensaries, the state instituted a 25 percent flat tax on purchases, effective January 1, 2016.

Measure 91 was silent with regard to municipalities' opting out of the commercial system. The state legislature subsequently approved a measure that would allow a municipality the choice of opting out if the municipality had voted no on Measure 91 with 55 percent or more of the vote. For all Oregonians, but particularly those in communities who opt out or those waiting for the recreational system to become operational, Measure 91 offers homegrows as an alternative and homegrowers may possess up to eight ounces of dried marijuana flower at one time and up to four plants. As in other states, public use is banned. Private establishments such as clubs cannot permit marijuana use on premises. Finally, the measure gives the legislature the power to change the relevant statutes (which the Oregon legislature took liberties to do early on) and gives substantial regulatory discretion to the Oregon Liquor Control Commission.

District of Columbia, 2014: Initiative 71

Washington, D.C., offers perhaps the most complicated situation in the legalization fight. On November 4, 2014, 65 percent of D.C. voters approved Initiative 71, legalizing marijuana possession and cultivation. However, under D.C.'s odd governance structure—shared power between the District government and the U.S. Congress—a D.C. ballot initiative cannot create a regulatory system within the District. Congress requires that such a system be established by the District Council. In this way, Initiative 71 laid the groundwork for a legal system, and the D.C.

Council would have to set up a market and regulatory apparatus post-passage.

As the Initiative 71 campaign got under way, members of the District Council began holding hearings and drafting legislation to set up the commercial market and regulatory structures, as most expected that the initiative would pass and marijuana would be legalized. But there is one catch: Congress has a thirty-day period in which it can "disapprove" or overturn any legislation or initiative passed in the District. This is the statutory avenue by which Congress can meddle in D.C. laws, as permitted under the District of Columbia Home Rule Act of 1973.

And there is another, more commonly used, means to meddle: Congress's budget power. Congress can refuse to allow the District government to use funds to enforce or implement a given law. In response to the passage of Initiative 71, that is precisely what Congress did. Representative Andy Harris (R-Md.) proposed an amendment to a bill that would have prevented the District from spending money to implement the initiative (set up and enforce a regulatory regime). In an omnibus budget deal later in 2014, the House inserted that language into the final bill that passed and was signed into law. The language remained in future budget deals.

The consequences of the Harris language did not overturn the initiative, but the District government could not implement it. So the District ended up with a legal home-grow system that the government could not, by law, regulate.

Thus, after an initiative campaign, a vote, and a waiting period in Congress, a budget deal created a situation in which D.C. "sort of" legalized marijuana.

THE FEDERAL RESPONSE TO LEGALIZATION EFFORTS When Colorado and Washington passed their legalization initiatives
in 2012, they created an additional legal gray area. Marijuana remained illegal under the Controlled Substances
Act, but—under the anticommandeering doctrine, which
has been upheld by the Supreme Court—the federal government cannot force a state government to enforce federal
law.[6] However, the feds did have other law enforcement
and judicial avenues to enforce the law or stop the states.
At the same time, the federal government had spent sixteen
years taking a largely hands-off approach to enforcing the
CSA with regard to states' medical marijuana programs
and had stood idly by as numerous states joined the medical marijuana ranks.

In fact, in response to the growing number of state-
regulated medical marijuana programs in the United
States and with the start of the Obama administration in
January 2009, Deputy Attorney General David Ogden issued what would become known as the Ogden Memo to
all U.S. Attorneys. It instructed federal prosecutors and
law enforcement to deprioritize using their resources to
enforce the CSA against medical marijuana programs that
were complying with the laws and regulations of their
states. This provided a partial reprieve from federal
intervention.

In 2012, Governors John Hickenlooper (D-Colo.) and
Jay Inslee (D-Wash.) wondered if that same type of reprieve
would also be extended to their recreational-use programs.
Shortly after passage of Amendment 64 and Initiative 502,
Attorney General Eric Holder signaled to governors a
similar approach to recreational marijuana: prioritizing

enforcement in key areas like dealing with drug cartels or sales to children. It was not the intent of the DOJ to go after states that developed and implemented a strong regulatory structure.[7] That informal conversation became more formal when the Justice Department issued guidance in August 2013 via a memo issued by Deputy Attorney General James Cole that outlined the enforcement priorities of the administration and suggested to federal prosecutors not to target state-law-compliant recreational marijuana programs in states that legalize and regulate.

The informal agreement—guidance and suggestion rather than a true legal solution—has largely held. Raids on growers still take place in Washington and Colorado, but generally in concert with local law enforcement investigations of people considered "bad actors" under the reformed system. The fear subsided among elected officials in the two early states that they could be subject to penalty or indictment for overseeing and being party to a massive drug operation that was technically illegal under federal law.

The Ogden and Cole Memos did not fix the system but instead patched it up with legal duct tape that covered over deep divisions between federal and state law. The Cole Memo partly was a reflection of a president and an administration with more lenient views on marijuana policy and partly was a political copout. The administration knew it could not effectively enforce the CSA against hundreds and eventually thousands of marijuana enterprises, let alone hundreds of thousands or millions of customers. Rather than look as though it had been defeated by states' efforts to reform marijuana laws, the administration took the face-saving approach of saying, "We have better things to do."

As Oregon, Alaska, and the District of Columbia legalized marijuana, the enforcement challenge for the administration grew even more difficult, making the Cole Memo more useful with each additional state that legalized. But the current standoff is untenable in the long run—and perhaps not possible in the short run, either. In the long run, issues still abound over banking, taxation, legality, interstate commerce, and a host of other challenges that arise because of the intersection of state and federal law. The Ogden and Cole Memos do nothing to address those challenges nor ameliorate the problems. In the shorter term, and as the clock runs out on the Obama administration, cannabis enterprises become more worried about what comes next. Memoranda like the ones holding together a fragile marijuana policy apparatus could be reversed and the War on Drugs ramped up again on the first day a new president takes office. The first battles in such a new war may well be in Alaska, Colorado, Oregon, Washington, and the District of Columbia.

PART V **THE FUTURE OF MARIJUANA**

THIRTEEN WEIGHING THE COSTS AND BENEFITS OF LEGALIZATION

THE UNITED STATES has had a remarkably unpredictable relationship with marijuana. Over the course of the nation's history, the plant has gone from a required crop to an accepted medical treatment to a government-regulated pharmaceutical to an illegal drug to a somewhat legal medicinal option to a locally legal and regulated substance.

Within the reform community there is disagreement as to whether marijuana use is a vice—but government treats it as one.[1] Marijuana's metamorphosis produced a patchwork of confusing, complex, and often contradictory laws at the federal, state, and local levels that at once deemed a substance illegal in all circumstances and simultaneously allowed people to buy it from a public storefront. As the twenty-first century proceeds, America will continue experimenting with marijuana policy. America is unsure whether it likes marijuana, but is willing to give it a chance. The country is unsure exactly what the best method to use it is, but it is trying a variety of options. It worries that there will be consequences, but recognizes there are benefits to be had. So America is giving marijuana a shot and hoping for the best.

Few things are certain, but we can be reasonably sure that states will learn from other states; that's already happened during the expansion of both medical and recreational programs. There will also be ups and downs with state systems. Some will get it right, others may do poorly, and there will likely be occasions of newsworthy situations that cast both positive and highly negative light on marijuana distribution and use. Public policy at its finest involves trial and error where jurisdictions function as laboratories until best practices gradually emerge and the system's functioning continues to improve. Improvement and refinement over time is an absolute necessity for marijuana policy, especially since it is very likely that state systems will only expand.

As more states legalize marijuana, there are some important ideas to highlight. It is generally acknowledged that legalizing marijuana entails some real risk. Any public policy change involves risk, and that is particularly true in an area in which public opinion is sharply divided, as it is on the use of an intoxicating substance and the expansion of legal access to that substance. Managing, minimizing, or otherwise handling those risks is an essential part of successful policy.

But it is also widely acknowledged that marijuana legalization provides tangible benefits. There is general consensus that marijuana prohibition has been a failure: it has not met its goal of a drug-free America, has been expensive, and has caused a great deal of collateral damage. Lives have been lost or derailed, millions have been arrested, and hundreds of thousands incarcerated for low-level crime, while criminal elements have been able to continue to wreak havoc upon the United States and other nations. Reforming the system in ways that put and end to the ongoing failures of the drug war would provide a substantial social benefit.

Legalization of marijuana can be seen as the leading edge of the marijuana reform community's success, but it is still too early to speak of a mature public policy on marijuana. There are still plenty of serious policy challenges and questions for the community to grapple with if the future is to include access to legal marijuana and if the policies around it are to succeed.

CONCERNS WITH LEGALIZATION   There are legitimate concerns about the results of legalization in the United States, but in discussing them it is important to avoid hysteria and outlandish fears, which are part of the legacy of the dishonest foundation for the drug wars. Marijuana will not turn users into murderers or force young women into promiscuity. Nor will users be transformed into derelicts, rapists, or psychopaths. However, we should also not let the zealotry of drug war rhetoric gloss over genuine issues that may arise—problems that if not addressed could shift public opinion and induce policy failure.

Increased Use and Potential Dependency
by Consumers

One such concern involves increased use as a result of legalization. People have known all along that marijuana exists and that there are ways to obtain it. Legalization doesn't induce discovery of the drug, but use could increase as access expands and the potential social costs (stigma, risk of arrest, worries over product quality) decrease. Reform advocates recognize that responsible use *should* increase for individuals who so choose. Yet, worries remain that people will overindulge or that children and youths may have increased access.

Polls suggest that under prohibition, youths have no problem accessing marijuana, and some surveys indicate that young people find it easier to get marijuana than alcohol. Reformers cite on the catchphrase "Dealers don't ask for an ID" to highlight the contrast between the illegal market and licensed, regulated dispensaries. Thus, a regulated market such as that for alcohol could make it somewhat more difficult for young people to obtain pot. Still, governments must closely monitor changes in youth use rates and, if increases occur, consider regulatory and educational steps that could diminish that problem.

Increases in adult use are also a legitimate concern. Even though the medical community has convincingly shown that marijuana is far less addicting than alcohol, tobacco, prescription narcotics, or other hard drugs, marijuana dependence is still a reality for some users. As legal access expands, governments must also monitor the incidence of dependence and work to curb it. Plans are in place in legalizing states to direct additional funding toward mental health and addiction services, but efforts must be made to ensure that such funding is sufficient.

Dependence of Industry on Increased Use

Connected to concerns about increased adult use is a worry about the industry's financial dependence on the heavy user. In the so-called vice industries—alcohol, tobacco, gambling—money is not made off those who occasionally indulge. Frequent gamblers, problem drinkers, and those addicted to tobacco deliver those respective industry profits. The same is true for marijuana. A recent report commissioned by the Colorado Department of Revenue, "Market Size and Demand for Marijuana in Colorado," estimated that frequent and heavy users, those who use marijuana more than twenty days a month, made up just 30 percent of the customer base but accounted for nearly 90 percent of the market demand. Government must ensure that industry is not capitalizing on and encouraging heavy users to use more.[2] Such a scenario can induce additional social costs and be seen as a manipulation of vulnerable individuals.

Public and Social Health Costs

Worry also exists that commercializing marijuana may cause a dramatic increase in the types of social and public health risks that the United States experiences from alcohol and tobacco use. Because vice companies tend to make more money from heavier users, and incentives exist to induce heavier use, such use will lead to increased public health and public safety risks. That has been true for tobacco, and it has been true for alcohol. Two caveats that exist to those worries focus on prohibition and marijuana's current place in society. The experience with alcohol prohibition did little to bring peace and social stability to America. Although the social ills of extreme alcohol abuse did decrease, the more punitive aspects of the regime gave rise to violence, organized crime, and other devastating social effects. In addition, arguments about social costs of heavier use that may result from marijuana legalization tend to ignore the prevalence of marijuana in society today. Marijuana abuse exists, and the United States is already bearing social costs from heavy users.

Concerns regarding social costs go beyond effects on the individual user. Robert Mikos, a professor at the Vanderbilt University Law School, argues that the patchwork access to legal marijuana where only some states and some communities allow access can create unintended or unexpected social costs.[3] He notes that people in prohibition jurisdictions will travel to legal jurisdictions to purchase marijuana. Sometimes they will use it in that legal jurisdiction, and sometimes they will (legally or illegally) return to their homes. Furthermore, prohibition jurisdictions will still incur social costs, but they cannot reap any of the social benefits—namely tax revenues and savings from reallocated law enforcement spending—to offset those costs. As legal marijuana expands, the negative effects of interstate patchwork access will diminish, but as long as states authorize municipal "opt-out" clauses, the intrastate effects will only increase.

Issues of localism go beyond social cost transfers. In states that have local opt-out provisions at either the county or municipal levels, choices are made about the marijuana market by local referendum or votes of local governing bodies such as city councils and county commissions. Local political battles can rage over these decisions. Often, counties and municipalities that opt out are clustered in rural and more conservative parts of states. Those choices can mean some live significantly far from legal dispensaries and can limit individuals' access to legal marijuana. In states without homegrows, such choices can enable continued black market behaviors in jurisdictions distant from legal markets.

Conflicts can also arise in places that allow for commercial grow sites and dispensaries, and NIMBY forces can take root even in liberal bastions in legal states. Some people are happy to embrace legalization as long as a dispensary isn't nearby. This leads to battles over zoning for marijuana enterprises. What often begins with conversations about keeping marijuana shops from schools and playgrounds becomes demand for keeping marijuana shops "away from me." These concerns are not minor, nor are they without merit. It is not hard to imagine how one's neighborhood might be affected by a dispensary setting up shop down the block. But these issues expose a reality many communities have awoken to: the passage of a legalization initiative does not end the policy conversation; it creates the landscape for a whole new set of policy issues, conversations, and fights.

Taxation and Other Financial Concerns

Another concern involves the impact of taxes and pricing on markets and social goals. In legal jurisdictions the base price of marijuana as well as the tax rate, which affects the price to the consumer, can create multiple complications. If the retail price is too high, the effort to displace the black market will be undermined. When marijuana is two or three times as expensive on the legal market as on the illegal market, many consumers will opt for the lower-priced pot because the benefits of legal pot (reduced risk of arrest and greater certainty over product quality) may not be perceived as outweighing the dollar cost. If the product is not properly priced, the legal and illegal market will continue to coexist. Governments can take steps to combat such a problem either by directly engaging in price controls or regulating the market in such a way that supply and tax rates lower the price enough to induce customers to access the legal market exclusively, or at least almost exclusively.

Prices that are too low also can have devastating effects. Prices can fall if the market is flooded with an oversupply of marijuana—good news for the displacement of the illegal market, but bad news for operators in the legal market. Base prices that are too low reduce business revenue and profit. Firms either have no profit incentive to stay in business or insufficient revenue to continue operating. That situation is further complicated by banking and taxation challenges that cannabis businesses face, which either drive up their costs of doing business or restrict their access to capital. In a period of low prices, larger ones are able to withstand the shock while smaller firms are driven out of business. Here again, government has a means of dealing with this situation: regulators can either engage directly in setting price floors or intervene to affect market dynamics in ways that restrict supply.

Regulatory Capture

Regulatory capture occurs when the entities that are supposed to be regulated end up being the ones calling the shots on the regulatory apparatus. The potential for regulatory capture increases as more states legalize marijuana and the industry matures. It would be disingenuous to say that there are no advantages to industry actors having an influence on regulators. In the early days of the legal marijuana industry, industry actors were essential players in regulatory processes. Since many growers and others had previous experience in the prelegalization environment, they had an information advantage over regulators who were brand-new to the marijuana game; government had to rely on industry for assistance in crafting regulations.

In Colorado, that relationship functioned well, at least out of the gate.[4] Over time, though, that scenario can threaten the legitimacy and effectiveness of those regulations. As the industry matures and possibly consolidates, that dynamic between industry and regulator can change such that the interests of industry are set above the public interest of effective regulation. Moving forward, legal states and states considering legalization must ensure that safeguards are in place in the regulatory process to ward off that kind of capture and ensure that the system functions according to the values of good government and that the benefits of legalization and regulation are balanced among the different stakeholders, including the cannabis industry.

THE BENEFITS OF MARIJUANA LEGALIZATION Obviously, most if not all of the many of the benefits associated with marijuana legalization (see chapter 12) cannot be realized until marijuana programs become operational.

Tax Revenues

Increased tax revenue is a big part of the sales pitch for legalization (although advocates have reported that the message was less effective with voters than was expected). Under prohibition, government could not reap the taxes and fees on the illegal commercial activity. Under legalization, states and municipalities can and do. In Colorado, according to the state's Department of Revenue, this meant about $135 million in revenue from taxes and fees in 2015 and another $58 million in the first four months of 2016. Even though it is a small amount as a percentage of the overall state budget, such a revenue stream is still significant enough to make an impact on public policy.

The new revenue flowing into state coffers is important, and so, too, is the way those tax dollars are spent. Each legal state selected a network of programs that marijuana taxes would support. Those programs vary dramatically across states, but each of those government activities has substantial or nearly universal public support. Marijuana taxes and fees support marijuana enforcement, school construction, education, transportation, research (often in public universities), mental health and addiction services, law enforcement, and more. Much of the funding is geared toward how each program deals with the impact of legal marijuana on its portfolio, and in that sense, states try to get marijuana to pay for itself—using revenue to offset additional government costs.

Regulatory Innovation

Regulatory innovation is another crucial area where governments benefit from marijuana legalization. In legal states, governments work to ensure that regulations are responsive to changing market dynamics, policy learning, and unexpected outcomes. Furthermore, systems were built into marijuana programs that sought to improve the ability of government to do its job. For example, Washington requires regular and extensive cost-benefit analyses in order to assess the impact of marijuana on that state and recommend ways to deal with costs incurred.[5] Across states, the use of seed-to-sale tracking is an effort to ensure that inventory remains traceable and is not diverted (when marijuana ends up in the hands of people who shouldn't have it). These systems can be "the backbone of [a state's] regulatory structure," and provide great value to regulators.[6] They are also innovative. The systems are constantly changing and being updated to meet the needs of industry actors and regulators, respond to changing market dynamics, and interface with new and existing technologies within the state. Such innovation helps ensure the security and safety of the supply chain and improves regulators' abilities to have a command over the system.

Legalizing marijuana induces market-based innovations as well as regulatory ones. The legal, private, competitive market ensures that industry actors are trying to beat their rivals, striving to come up with the "next big thing"—honing cutting-edge cultivation techniques, dreaming up new ways to consume and market marijuana, or developing new cannabis strains for new purposes. Some of these innovations are utter failures, but others can be game changers, transforming the industry and consumers' relationship to it. That type of innovation is often stymied in a risky, closed, illegal market.

Another aspect of both private market and regulatory innovation involves product safety. Product testing only takes place in a legal market and is enhanced by a regulated one. Many medical- and recreational-legal states require firms to test the products they sell for potency, composition, and adulteration. Product testing is often combined with strict rules for growing conditions, ensuring not only the purity of the product (no chemicals, mold, or other bacteria are present) but also its strength (how much THC the marijuana contains). Several states were slow to get their testing programs off the ground. For example, it took Colorado months before an effective product testing system was in place.[7] Now, it is the standard in legal states to ensure that producers and consumers are fully informed about what is being sold.

Broader Economic Benefits

Economic benefits in addition to increased tax revenues have flowed to states under legalization. Primary, secondary, and tertiary marijuana markets have grown economies, created jobs, generated profits, delivered tax revenue, and pushed entrepreneurs to give back to their community. They have brought people with marijuana-growing skills out of the shadows of prohibition and given them gainful employment (and they pay income tax). In 2015 alone, Colorado issued over 25,000 licenses to work in the marijuana industry. Some of those licenses will go unused or will expire (as people exit the industry), but that number does not directly measure the number of jobs created in the growing marijuana industry. So the impact on the labor force is actually greater than the number of licenses would suggest because each licensed enterprise employs multiple individuals, as do enterprises in the secondary markets that the marijuana industry relies on.

For the tourism industry, legal adult-use marijuana has been a boon. People travel from prohibition states to legal states in order to use the product without having legal worries. A 2015 report from the Colorado Tourism Office suggested that summer visitors to the state were influenced heavily by the state's legal status, ensuring additional tourism funds flow into a state that relies significantly on tourism as a source of revenue.

As legal marijuana expands within states, markets stabilize, prices find a happy equilibrium, and, perhaps more important, as more states join the legalization ranks, the system becomes serious competition for the illegal market and international drug operations. Both supporters and opponents of legalization want to see the elimination of the illegal drug market. No one wants international drug cartels, gangs, or common drug dealers to operate in his or her community. Opponents of legalization look to prohibition to eliminate illegal markets—a goal that prohibition has totally failed. Supporters predict that legalization has a better chance to displace illegal markets. The jury is still out, but some early evidence suggests that cartels and other illegal operators have lost influence in legal states.[8]

Positive Effects of Legalization on Criminal Justice

Last but definitely not least, the legalization of marijuana has significant positive effects for criminal justice. Advancing racial justice is one of the goals of the legalization movement and one of the most central justifications for supporting legalization initiatives. Data from marijuana-legal states show dramatic decreases in marijuana offenses—which is logical and to be expected.[9] The *Washington Post* reported that in Colorado, the number of marijuana arrests in 2014 was just 5 percent of what is was in 2011, having dropped from 39,027 to 2,036.[10] A reduction of 37,000 arrests in a single state every year has enormous significance to people's personal lives and hence to society at large. A marijuana arrest— even a simple possession arrest—is a stigma that lingers for a person's entire life. Prosecution and jail sentences impact people's educational and housing opportunities, job prospects, health, social situation, and right to vote.

As legal states dramatically decrease the number of individuals being arrested for marijuana offenses, lives are changed and improved, and one must assume that some individuals' entire paths are being diverted toward greater success and less trouble. Such a change can happen for someone simply because the joint in his pocket or the bag of bud in his jacket no longer lands him in lockup.

LOOKING INTO THE CANNABIS CRYSTAL BALL   As marijuana legalization proceeds, new issues will arise and the pressure to deal with existing issues will increase. How local, state, and federal governments as well as international bodies deal with these challenges and questions will determine the future success of marijuana legalization policy.

By the beginning of 2016 in the United States, four states legalized marijuana and for the first time, two states that share a border legalized—Washington and Oregon. Studying how that border influences the market and consumer behavior will be an interesting challenge. Of course it is against federal law to transport marijuana bought in one state to the other (in fact, it is still against federal law to possess that marijuana in the first place). But the reality on the ground is that the state border will be porous and product will move across it. Competition between bordering states will influence public policy and will have an impact on the likelihood of marijuana crossing state lines.

One can imagine states quietly but purposefully engaging in pricing wars in an effort to entice additional consumers, even if those consumers are not supposed to "purchase here and go there." As more states legalize, the challenge of controlling (or deciding not to control) cross-border transport will become greater. As the 2016 elections proceed, Nevada, California, and Arizona all have robust drives to put legalization initiatives on their ballots. If all pass it will create a substantial western bloc of marijuana-legal states.[11] Such a dynamic will almost certainly induce such price wars, and states as well as the federal government will need to think about how best to respond, either to prevent such behaviors or accept that such behaviors result from market forces that are here to stay.

The spread of marijuana legalization is not a strictly American phenomenon. For some time, the Netherlands was the world's most progressive pot paradise. Since the mid-1970s the Netherlands has had an odd system that provides marijuana to customers at specific cafes, under an agreement that functions as a type of storefront decriminalization. However, the production and processing of marijuana remain illegal, meaning the legal café market must still rely on an illegal grow market. Such a system involves layers of tolerance from government institutions in allowing the market to exist.

In 2013, Uruguay became the world's first nation to fully legalize marijuana. The government authorized commercial growers to supply marijuana to pharmacies, and they could dispense marijuana to (nonmedical) customers. The program also authorized homegrows and cooperatives. In a cooperative, people come together and pool resources to grow a larger supply of marijuana, but each member of the co-op is entitled only to a maximum amount of marijuana monthly. Under the Uruguayan model, consumers must register with the government and can only access marijuana through one of those avenues. Despite the 2013 reform, by the beginning of 2016, the Uruguayan system had not yet gotten off the ground owing to delays in implementation.

In Canada, parliamentary elections in 2015 made Justin Trudeau, the son of the late Prime Minister Pierre Trudeau, the nation's twenty-third prime minister. Shortly after his win, Trudeau instructed the Canadian bureaucracy to prepare to legalize, regulate, and provide access to marijuana, a policy his administration would pursue actively. Canada legalized medical marijuana through a series of court decisions in the early 2000s, and Trudeau made it his mission to move Canada toward wider reforms.

How other nations and international organizations respond to marijuana reform will have a tremendous impact on the future of such policy. As leading global nations like Canada or the United States take more reform-oriented approaches to marijuana, it will surely push the international community toward acceptance or at least tolerance. Also, depending on their responses, international organizations could also push other, more reform-oriented nations toward legalization. In much the same way that efforts in Colorado and Washington spurred greater reform in other American states, national-level legalization may well spur such contagious reforms across the globe.

The one key institution to watch in this process is the United Nations. The UN currently maintains the international standard on drug prohibition via the Single Convention on Narcotic Drugs. The Single Convention remained in place even as nations and American states began to reform their laws. The UN response to this situation could affect nations' future legalization decisions, particularly those of smaller, less-powerful nations. It could also affect the UN's own legitimacy. If the response is one of strong and vocal opposition to legalization, and nations continue to legalize despite it, it will put into stark contrast the limited enforcement power the international organization has over policy across the world.

In a similar fashion, the authority of the U.S. government is challenged as more states opt to pursue recreational legalization. As the number of legal states grows, it becomes harder for the federal government to enforce the Controlled Substances Act. At the same time, the shared legal authority of federal and state governments continues to hamper the cannabis industry's efficient functioning.

The resulting situation in the United States may be worse than either national legalization or national prohibition. Legal realities are loosely defined by executive branch guidance and suggestions from the administration. That guidance fails to answer important questions and oftentimes creates new ones. States are constantly asking the federal government how to deal with many of the problems they face; the answers are almost always insufficient. Members of Congress have proposed solutions to some of the biggest challenges facing states, industry actors, and customers, but that legislation is not acted on. The reality is that the state of American law at the start of 2016 is absolutely untenable and is inconsistent with American principles of fairness and equal treatment. Federal officials must commit themselves to coherent, comprehensive, and sensible marijuana policy. Until they do, the system will be arbitrary and unjust, and policy will be ineffective.

This incoherent state of affairs influences many topics that demand a decisive federal policy response. One of the most troubling of these issues for the cannabis industry is banking. Under federal law, marijuana enterprises are engaging in an illegal trade, which makes them ineligible to access standard financial products that banks offer: checking accounts, savings accounts, lines of credit, business loans, and so forth. Consequently, most marijuana businesses are forced to resort to a cash-only operation. Cash-only businesses create tremendous security risks for firms, their employees, and their customers and make regulatory auditing of firms more difficult. A cash-only system creates a seriously risky business environment and offers bad actors opportunities for money laundering. Those risks are held in place by a government that refuses to implement a policy fix.

One effort to solve the banking problem came on Valentine's Day, 2014, in the form of a "guidance" from the Department of Treasury conveying to financial institutions the manner in which they could interact with marijuana businesses. But a love letter it was not. The guidance was vague and did not offer financial institutions sufficient protection against federal action under the Banking Secrecy

Act. The industry felt the guidance was not enough to let banks engage with these businesses, so this action by the Treasury did nothing to solve the problem.

For businesses, the tax problem can be just as troubling. Under U.S. tax law, specifically Section 280E of the Internal Revenue Code, any company that traffics in a Schedule I or Schedule II substance is not entitled to business tax deductions. However, the tax code requires all businesses, even illegal ones, to file business tax returns. In order to comply with existing state and federal laws, marijuana enterprises file tax returns annually. Under an agreement with the federal government, firms who file taxes—and thus notify the federal government they exist as a business in violation of federal law—will not be targeted for prosecution, unless they commit tax fraud or evasion. The paradox is that marijuana businesses are responsible for all of the standard business taxes, but are ineligible for the same deductions that other American businesses are entitled to. The result is a revenue problem for these firms, as tax burdens can be tremendous. Some young firms report having tax burdens in excess of 100 percent of revenue—an unsustainable operating environment. Legislators, advocates, and state officials have pleaded with the federal government to reform tax laws. These groups argue that if the federal government is tacitly allowing marijuana enterprises to exist, they should also treat them like other businesses for the purposes of taxation. Until the federal government provides a solution, federal tax policy will unnecessarily burden the entire marijuana industry.

Another aspect of the industry that will be important to watch involves growth and consolidation, and how government responds to it. As the marijuana industry matures and as more states, and nations, reform their laws to permit recreational marijuana, market dynamics can change. One worry in advocacy communities is the possible advent of Big Marijuana—the rise of national and perhaps eventually multinational corporations, as occurred in the tobacco industry. Marijuana is a capital-intensive agricultural product that is produced, processed, and sold in similar ways to tobacco products, so concerns about market structure are not unfounded. Could a Philip Morris of marijuana dominate the industry and engage in bad practices and regulatory capture? In the case of Big Tobacco, for decades the industry's political power combined with widespread consumer addiction and use allowed corporations to manipulate and hide scientific evidence about the addictive properties and health effects of and carcinogenic compounds in and added to tobacco.

Similar worries concerning marijuana are thus justified, yet, after the Big Tobacco lesson, many people are sensitive to that dynamic in advance. What is more likely is that if a large corporation emerges from the pack, it would face unprecedented scrutiny from both government regulators and industry competitors. That scrutiny could help blunt the type of formal and informal market power that Philip Morris enjoyed. Moreover, aware of the potential for a marijuana powerhouse to dominate the industry, state regulators have armed themselves with a variety of tools to limit the power of such a firm.

As those new, large firms emerge in the marijuana industry, it will be important to see whether those firms have higher rates of regulatory compliance than smaller firms. Those firms may also drive efficiencies and scale and improve market conditions and stability. It will be important to see how large firms behave and participate in the economic arena and whether large marijuana enterprises are known more for the benefits or the risks that corporate consolidation can offer.

The final item to watch in the future is research. Research is essential to the formulation of responsible marijuana policy, including studies of medical marijuana's efficacy and safety and of the social, public health, and public safety implications of recreational marijuana. There is not a single corner of the marijuana policy world that cannot be aided by additional analysis. There are two things we should consider.

First, will state, federal, and international governments expand their support of medical marijuana research? Prohibition has rested on what I have called medical marijuana's trifecta of prohibition in the CSA: the three assertions that marijuana has no medicinal value, is not safe for medical treatment, and has a high risk for abuse. Research must continue to put those claims to the test, and if they are effectively refuted—which many would argue has already happened—government institutions must revise their designation of marijuana.

Second, how will the public respond to new findings on the social impacts of marijuana? U.S. jurisdictions that have legalized recreational marijuana have funded studies or committed to supporting work on a variety of questions about the impact of the substance on their communities. As data and findings pour in from this work, it will be important to understand both the positive and negative impacts and, further, to study public opinion and communities' responses. Results are unlikely to be black and white—neither everything right nor everything wrong. This research will most likely generate policy recommendations about how to tighten regulations, improve systems, and protect public interests. The willingness of states to adopt such recommendations will be critical to anchoring the legitimacy and effectiveness of marijuana programs and to ensuring sustained public support for legalized marijuana.

A federal policy response is inevitable. It may come in the form of discrete reforms that ultimately mold a broader system, or it may be sweeping in nature. The choices the federal government must and will make will have far-reaching consequences. Will the government proceed with incremental medical marijuana reform or will it accept medical and recreational systems in one fell swoop? The former is probably more likely, given the positions of many members of Congress and a history of presidents hesitant to be aggressive reformers.

What might federal marijuana reforms look like? Will they involve significant federal power? Will the federal government take a largely hands-off, states' rights approach, or will reform resemble alcohol regulation: broad federal standards supplemented by state power to regulate many aspects of the industry? Such a reform plan would have hugely disruptive effects in existing marijuana-legal states. Currently a state's medical and recreational marijuana systems tend to look quite similar, but systems across states vary dramatically. Federal intervention and reform could cause upheaval in states forced to implement dramatic regulatory, administrative, budgetary, and market changes to comply with federal laws. Consistent federal marijuana reform will provide numerous benefits, but there will be a lengthy adaptation period in which state systems and the doctors, patients, consumers, growers, business owners, regulators, and others will face significant challenges.

Future marijuana policy is the object of cautious hope. It will almost certainly involve more jurisdictions embracing legal marijuana for a variety of reasons. At the same time, such policy reforms will also come with risks and challenges. The response of governments, industry actors, consumers, and the public will determine the outlines of both the success and expansion of such reforms. Most Americans and many outside the country look at marijuana prohibition and see it as failed public policy. At the same time, many observers are skeptical that full-scale legalization is the right response. The United States and other countries are taking slow steps to figure out how to recover from the consequences of a failed drug war. The spread of full-scale legalization to more American states may be the best precondition for creating the laboratories of democracy where workable marijuana policies will be tested.

NOTES

Chapter One

1. Lucas Laursen, "Botany: The Cultivation of Weed," *Nature* 525, no. 7570 (www.nature.com/nature/journal/v525/n7570_supp/full/525S4a.html).

2. Lyle E. Craker and Zoe Gardener, "The Botany of Cannabis," in *The Pot Book: A Complete Guide to Cannabis*, ed. Julie Holland (Rochester, Vt.: Park Street Press), p. 38.

3. Ibid.

4. Robert Clarke, *Marijuana Botany: An Advanced Study* (Berkeley, Calif.: Ronan, 1981).

5. Danny Danko, "Cannabis Grow Revolution," in Holland, *Pot Book,* pp. 73–130.

6. Roger Nicoll and Bradley Alger, "The Brain's Own Marijuana," *Scientific American,* December 2004, pp. 69–75.

7. Maureen Dowd, "Don't Harsh Our Mellow, Dude," *New York Times,* op-ed, June 3, 2014.

8. Julie Holland, "The Government's Pot Farm," in Holland, *Pot Book*, chapter 23.

9. See Caleb Hellerman, "Is Super Weed, Super Bad?" CNN (website), August 9, 2013 (www.cnn.com/2013/08/09/health/weed-potency-levels/).

10. Martin A. Lee, *Smoke Signals: A Social History of Marijuana—Medical, Recreational, and Scientific* (New York: Scribner, 2012), p. 6.

11. Matt Thompson, "The Mysterious History of 'Marijuana,'" National Public Radio broadcast, July 23, 2013 (www .npr.org/sections/codeswitch/2013/07/14/201981025/the -mysterious-history-of-marijuana).

12. Harry J. Anslinger, "Marijuana, Assassin of Youth," *American Magazine* 124, no. 1 (1964).

13. Eugene Stanley, "Marihuana as a Developer of Criminals," *American Journal of Political Science* 2 (1931), p. 252.

14. Ibid.

Chapter Two

1. See website for U.S. Pharmacopeial Convention, "USP-NF" (www.usp.org/usp-nf).

2. "An Act to provide for the registration of, with collectors of internal revenue, and to impose a special tax upon all persons who produce, import, manufacture, compound, deal in, dispense, sell, distribute, or give away opium or coca leaves, their salts, derivatives, or preparations, and for other purposes." See Edward M. Brecher and the Editors of Consumer Reports Magazine, *The Consumer's Union Report on Licit and Illicit Drugs,* "Chapter 8. The Harrison Narcotic Act, 1914" (www.druglibrary .org/schaffer/library/studies/cu/cu8.html; accessed May 16, 2016).

3. Much of this early tax-centered drug control policy predated the passage of the Sixteenth Amendment, in 1913, which authorized the collection of a federal income tax. The Harrison Act was passed in 1914.

4. It became Public Law 71-357 when President Herbert Hoover signed it into law on June 14, 1930.

5. Douglas Valentine, *The Strength of the Wolf* (London: Verso, 2004).

6. Kathleen J. Frydl, *The Drug Wars in America, 1940–1973* (New York: Cambridge University Press, 2013), p. 30.

7. Harry J. Anslinger, "Marijuana, Assassin of Youth," *The American Magazine* 124, no. 1 (July 1937).

8. Ibid.

9. Ibid.

10. The Food, Drug, and Cosmetic Act of 1938 amended and overhauled the Pure Food and Drug Act of 1906 (Federal Food and Drugs Act of 1906).

11. "The Marihuana Problem in the City of New York," Mayor's Committee on Marihuana, New York Academy of Medicine, New York, 1944.

12. Anslinger quoted in Lee, *Smoke Signals*, pp. 61, 62.

Chapter Three

1. For the complete text of the report, see United Nations Office on Drugs and Crime, "Report of the Interdepartmental Committee on Narcotics to the President of the United States, January 1, 1956" (https://www.unodc.org/unodc/en/data-and-analysis /bulletin/bulletin_1956-01-01_2_page003.html; accessed May 16, 2016).

2. Ibid., "Recommendations."

3. Ibid. In fact, the eighth recommendation of the Eisenhower report states that "progress towards full and effective international controls over the production and distribution of the narcotic drugs was felt by the Committee to have been highly encouraging. It recommended that the United States Government continue its policy of close co-operative effort through the agency of the United Nations, and with other international groups and individual nations concerned with the problem."

4. The Convention took effect in 1964 and was approved by the United States on May 25, 1967.

5. United Nations Office on Drugs and Crime, "The International Drug Control Conventions" (www.unodc.org/documents /commissions/CND/Int_Drug_Control_Conventions/Ebook/The _International_Drug_Control_Conventions_E.pdf, p. 47).

6. See Valentine, *Strength of the Wolf.*

7. Drug Abuse Control Amendments of 1965 became Public Law 89-74.

8. Despite the transfer of some responsibilities to the FDA, much of the authority over drug control policy remained with law enforcement agencies.

Chapter Four

1. Ehrlichman quoted in Dan Baum, "Legalize It All," *Harper's,* April 13, 2016 (http://harpers.org/archive/2016/04 /legalize-it-all/).

2. Richard Nixon, "Special Message to the Congress on the Control of Narcotics and Dangerous Drugs, July 14, 1969," The American Presidency Project (www.presidency.ucsb.edu/ws/?pid =2126).

3. Ibid.

4. Ibid.

5. 395 U.S. 6 (1969).

6. For an extended discussion of Operation Intercept, the Mexican government's response, and the fallout from the effort, see Frydl, *Drug Wars in America,* pp. 377–80.

7. Richard Nixon, "Remarks at a Bipartisan Leadership Meeting on Narcotics and Dangerous Drugs, October 23, 1969," The American Presidency Project (www.presidency.ucsb.edu/ws /?pid=2280; accessed May 16, 2016).

8. See Frydl, *Drug Wars in America,* pp. 377–80.

9. Public Law 91-513.

10. Richard Nixon, "Remarks on Signing the Comprehensive Drug Abuse Prevention and Control Act of 1970, October 27, 1970," The American Presidency Project (www.presidency.ucsb .edu/ws/?pid=2767; accessed May 17, 2016).

11. Richard Nixon, "Remarks about an Intensified Program for Drug Abuse Prevention and Control 17, June 17, 1971," The American Presidency Project (www.presidency.ucsb.edu/ws/?pid =3047; accessed May 17, 2016).

12. Richard Nixon, "Special Message to the Congress on Drug Abuse Prevention and Control, June 17, 1971," The American Presidency Project (www.presidency.ucsb.edu/ws/?pid=3048; accessed May 17, 2016).

13. Codified as Public Law 92-255. For the details of the House and Senate votes, see Govtrack.us (www.govtrack.us /congress/votes/92-1972/h368; www.govtrack.us/congress/votes /92-1971/s398).

Chapter Five

1. Section 601(e) of the CSA says: "The Commission shall conduct a comprehensive study and investigation of the causes of drug abuse and their relative significance. The Commission shall submit to the President and the Congress such interim reports as it deems advisable and shall within two years after the date on which funds first become available to carry out this section submit to the President and the Congress a final report which shall contain a detailed statement of its findings and conclusions and also recommendations for legislation and administrative actions as it deems appropriate.

2. Congressional Record, House of Representatives, September 24, 1970, p. 33617.

3. More than $6 million in 2015 dollars.

4. National Commission on Marihuana and Drug Abuse, "Marihuana: A Signal of Misunderstanding," chapter 5 (www .druglibrary.org/schaffer/library/studies/nc/ncrec2.htm).

5. Richard Nixon, Oval Office Conversation No. 568-4 (www.csdp.org/research/nixonpot.txt).

6. Richard Nixon, News Conference, March 24, 1972, The American Presidency Project (www.presidency.ucsb.edu/ws/index .php?pid=3356; accessed May 17, 2016).

7. Richard Nixon, "Campaign Statement about Crime and Drug Abuse, October 28, 1972," The American Presidency Project (www.presidency.ucsb.edu/ws/?pid=3665; accessed May 17, 2016).

8. Richard Nixon, "State of the Union Message to the Congress on Law Enforcement and Drug Abuse Prevention, March 14, 1973," The American Presidency Project (www.presidency.ucsb .edu/ws/?pid=4140; accessed May 17, 2016).

9. Richard Nixon, "Message to the Congress Transmitting Reorganization Plan 2 of 1973 Establishing the Drug Enforcement Administration, March 28, 1973," The American Presidency Project (www.presidency.ucsb.edu/ws/?pid=4159; accessed May 17, 2016).

10. See the DEA website, "DEA Staffing & Budget" (www.dea .gov/about/history/staffing.shtml; accessed May 17, 2016).

11. Ibid. Between 2012 and 2013, as part of sequestration under the Budget Control Act of 2011, the DEA's budget was

reduced by about 3 percent, to $91 million. In 2014 those budget cuts were restored and the DEA budget grew to exceed 2012 levels.

12. Gerald Ford, "Special Message to Congress on Drug Abuse, April 27, 1976," The American Presidency Project (www.presidency.ucsb.edu/ws/?pid=5875; accessed May 17, 2016).

13. Gerald Ford, "Statement on Receiving the Report of the Domestic Council Drug Abuse Task Force, October 14, 1975," The American Presidency Project (www.presidency.ucsb.edu/ws/?pid=5325; accessed May 17, 2016).

14. The Office of Drug Abuse Policy was established on March 19, 1976, with the passage of a law amending the Drug Abuse Office and Treatment Act of 1972 (P.L. 94-237). The 1972 law (P.L. 92-255) initially created the Special Action Office for Drug Abuse Prevention (Sec. 201).

15. All the following quotes on President Carter's drug policy are from Jimmy Carter, "Drug Abuse Message to the Congress, August 2, 1977," The American Presidency Project (www.presidency.ucsb.edu/ws/?pid=7908; accessed May 17, 2016).

Chapter Six

1. Ronald Reagan, "Radio Address to the Nation on Federal Drug Policy, October 2, 1982," The American Presidency Project (www.presidency.ucsb.edu/ws/?pid=43085; accessed May 17, 2016).

2. Gil Troy, *Morning in America: How Ronald Reagan Invented the 1980s* (Princeton University Press, 2007).

3. Ronald Reagan, "Remarks on Signing Executive Order 12368, Concerning Federal Drug Abuse Policy Functions, June 24, 1982," The American Presidency Project (www.presidency.ucsb.edu/ws/index.php?pid=42671%23axzz1P5p1SnqO; accessed May 17, 2016).

4. Public Laws 98-473, 99-570, and 100-690.

5. George H. W. Bush, "Address to the Nation on the National Drug Control Strategy, September 5, 1989," The American Presidency Project (www.presidency.ucsb.edu/ws/?pid=17472; accessed May 17, 2016).

6. United Nations Office on Drugs and Crime, "Report of the Interdepartmental Committee on Narcotics to the President

of the United States, January 1, 1956" (https://www.unodc.org /unodc/en/data-and-analysis/bulletin/bulletin_1956-01-01_2 _page003.html; accessed May 17, 2016).

7. Partnership for Drug-Free Kids, "What We Do" (www .drugfree.org/about/about-us/; accessed May 17, 2016).

8. "This Is Your Brain on Drugs," video (www.youtube.com /watch?v=ub_a2t0ZfTs).

9. Ruth C. Engs and Stuart W. Fors, "Drug Abuse Hysteria: The Challenge of Keeping Perspective," *Journal of School Health* 58, no. 1 (1988), pp. 26–28.

10. Steven L. West and Keri K. O'Neal, "Project D.A.R.E. Outcome Effectiveness Revisited," *American Journal of Public Health* 94, no. 6 (2004), pp. 1027–29; Wei Pan and Haiyan Bai, "A Multivariate Approach to Meta-Analytic Review of the Effectiveness of the D.A.R.E. Program," *International Journal of Environmental Research and Public Health* 6, no. 1 (2009), pp. 267–77.

11. Public Law 103-322.

12. The Edward Byrne Memorial Justice Assistance Grant Program.

13. Ryan King and Marc Mauer, "The War on Marijuana: The Transformation of the War on Drugs in the 1990s," *Harm Reduction Journal* 3, no. 6 (2006) (https://harmreductionjournal .biomedcentral.com/articles/10.1186/1477-7517-3-6).

Chapter Seven

1. "Presidential Approval," Roper Center for Public Opinion Research (http://ropercenter.cornell.edu/polls/presidential -approval/).

2. "Ridge: Bush Officials Sought to Raise Terror Alert before '04 Vote," CNN Online (www.cnn.com/2009/POLITICS /08/21/ridge.terror.level/; accessed May 17, 2016).

3. See Pew Research Center, "Why Americans Support or Oppose Legalizing Marijuana," Survey (Washington, D.C.: Pew Research Center, April 14, 2015). Regarding the Gallup survey, a direct yes-or-no question on legalization lacks nuance and can be polarizing. The data on responses are included here because these data are the best we have—the question has been asked consistently for nearly fifty years. In addition, despite the lack of nuance,

responses to the question do provide some insight into public perceptions. One might expect support for other moderate reforms like medical marijuana or decriminalization would be higher than 12 percent, but those topics were not polled. See Jeffrey M. Jones, "In U.S., 58% Back Legal Marijuana Use," Gallup (website), October 21, 2015 (www.gallup.com/poll/186260/back-legal-marijuana.aspx).

4. Ibid.

5. Pew Research Center, "In Debate over Legalizing Marijuana, Disagreement over Drug's Dangers," April 14, 2015 (www.people-press.org/2015/04/14/in-debate-over-legalizing-marijuana-disagreement-over-drugs-dangers/; accessed May 17, 2016).

6. While members of the greatest generation were polled, they composed too small of a subset for accurate cross-tabs.

7. Art Swift, "For the First Time, Americans Favor Legalizing Marijuana," Gallup (website), October 22, 2013 (www.gallup.com/poll/165539/first-time-americans-favor-legalizing-marijuana.aspx; accessed January 29, 2016).

8. Ibid.

9. In 1975, the Alaska Supreme Court ruled, in *Ravin v. State of Alaska,* that residents had the right to grow marijuana on their own property for personal use under right-to-privacy provisions in the Alaska constitution. This ruling stood until a 1990 ballot initiative reversed the decision. See Chief Justice Rabinowitz, "Opinion" (https://scholar.google.com/scholar_case?case=6713928512369047560&hl=en&as_sdt=6&as_vis=1&oi=scholar). See also Emi Sasagawa, "Marijuana in Alaska Has Long Been Legal. Now the State Is Struggling to Regulate It," *Govbeat* (blog), July 17, 2015 (www.washingtonpost.com/blogs/govbeat/wp/2015/07/17/marijuana-in-alaska-has-long-been-legal-now-the-state-is-struggling-to-regulate-it/; accessed May 17, 2016).

10. For 1999 Gallup poll results, see Mark Gillespie, "Americans Support Legalization of Marijuana for Medical Use" (www.gallup.com/poll/2902/americans-support-legalization-marijuana-medicinal-use.aspx). For 2003, 2005, and 2010 Gallup poll results, see Gallup, "Illegal Drugs" (www.gallup.com/poll/1657/illegal-drugs.aspx).

11. Gallup's question was "Would you favor or oppose making marijuana legally available for doctors to prescribe in order to reduce pain and suffering?" See Gallup, "Illegal Drugs."

12. See PollingReport.com, "Illegal Drugs" (www.pollingreport.com/drugs.htm).

13. It is important to note that majority support for a ballot initiative does not mean there is majority support statewide, as those results do not necessarily reflect the views of the population at large.

14. Marijuana Policy Project, "Support for Marijuana Policy Reform," see "State-specific medical marijuana public opinion polling results" (www.mpp.org/support-for-marijuana-policy-reform/; accessed May 17, 2016).

15. Ibid.

16. See Cornell University, Roper Center for Public Opinion Research, "Presidential Approval: Obama Presidential Approval" (https://ropercenter.cornell.edu/polls/presidential-approval/).

17. Gallup (website), "Congress and the Public" (www.gallup.com/poll/1600/congress-public.aspx).

18. Ibid.

19. Gallup (website), "Supreme Court" (www.gallup.com/poll/4732/supreme-court.aspx).

20. Gallup (website), "Confidence in Institutions" (www.gallup.com/poll/1597/confidence-institutions.aspx).

Chapter Eight

1. See Ernest L. Abel, *Marijuana: The First Twelve Thousand Years* (New York: Springer, 1980), chapter 4; George Washington's Mount Vernon (website), "George Washington Grew Hemp (but Not the Kind You're Thinking Of . . ." (www.mountvernon.org/george-washington/the-man-the-myth/george-washington-grew-hemp); Th. Jefferson Monticello (website), "Some of my finest hours have been spent on my back veranda, smoking hemp . . . (Quotation)" (www.monticello.org/site/jefferson/some-my-finest-hours-have-been-spent-my-back-veranda-smoking-hemp-quotation).

2. Corliss K. Engle, "John Adams, Farmer and Gardener," *Arnoldia* 61, no. 4 (2002), pp. 9–14.

3. "Uncle Sam Will Buy $69 Million Worth of Pot from Ole Miss," *Time,* March 23, 2015.

4. For Marx, see Martin Chilton, "Groucho Marx: 10 Things You Might Not Know," *The Telegraph*, August 19, 2015 (www.telegraph.co.uk/comedy/comedians/groucho-marx -profile-things-you-might-not-know/); for Flynn, see Thomas McNulty, *Errol Flynn: The Life and Career* (Jefferson, N.C.: Mc-Farland, 2011); for Mitchum, see Scott Harrison, "Robert Mitchum's 1948 Arrest on Marijuana Charges," Framework, *Los Angeles Times*, October 7, 2014 (http://framework.latimes.com /2014/10/07/robert-mitchums-1948-arrest-on-marijuana-charges /#/0).

5. James Fell, "Montel Williams Confronts MS Head On," *Los Angeles Times*, May 5, 2012.

6. "Richard Branson Admits: 'I Smoked Drugs with My Son,'" *Daily Mail*, July 30, 2007 (www.dailymail.co.uk/news /article-471730/Richard-Branson-admits-I-smoked-drugs-son .html; accessed May 17, 2016).

7. Jane Wells, "Men's Wearhouse Founder Comes Out in Favor of Pot Legalization," CNBC, September 19, 2015 (www .cnbc.com/2015/09/18/mens-wearhouse-founder-comes-out-in -favor-of-pot-legalization.html).

8. Jennifer Steinhauer, "Bloomberg Says He Regrets Marijuana Remarks," *New York Times*, April 10, 2002.

9. Robert Deitch, *Hemp: American History Revisited* (New York: Algora, 2003).

10. Ronald Reagan, "Remarks Announcing the Nomination of Douglas H. Ginsburg to Be an Associate Justice of the United States Supreme Court," October 29, 1987 (www.reagan.utexas .edu/archives/speeches/1987/102987g.htm; accessed May 18, 2016).

11. Keith Love, "Candidates Gore, Babbitt Admit Past Use of Marijuana," *Los Angeles Times*, November 8, 1987.

12. Katharine Q. Seelye, "Barack Obama, Asked about Drug History, Admits He Inhaled," *New York Times*, October 24, 2006.

Chapter Nine

1. Albert DiChiara and John F. Galliher, in "Dissonance and Contradiction in the Origins of Marihuana Decriminalization," *Law & Society Review* 28, no. 1 (1994), pp. 41–78, pro-

vide an excellent overview of this history of state-level decriminalization measures. Alaska's decriminalization of marijuana resulted from a state supreme court ruling that persons had the right to grow for their personal use on their property. Although New York decriminalized formally in 1977, the law was not enforced in New York City until 2014.

Chapter Ten

1. "American Public Health Association Endorses Medical Use of Marijuana," 104th Congress, 1st Session, *Congressional Record* 141, no. 199 (www.congress.gov/congressional-record /1995/12/14/extensions-of-remarks-section/article/E2365-2).

2. For a list of the bill's sponsors, see Congress.gov (www .congress.gov/bill/97th-congress/house-bill/4498/cosponsors? q=percent7B percent22search percent22 percent3A percent5B percent22 percent5C percent22marijuana percent5C percent22 percent22 percent5D percent7D&resultIndex=23; accessed May 18, 2016).

3. House Amendment 748 was attached to H.R. 4660, the Commerce, Justice, Science, and Related Agencies Appropriations Act of 2015 (www.congress.gov/amendment/113th-congress /house-amendment/748?q=percent7B percent22search percent22 percent3A percent5B percent22marijuana percent22 percent5D percent7D&resultIndex=12; accessed May 18, 2016).

4. Part of this section draws on research I conducted with Grace Wallack. See John Hudak and Grace Wallack, "How to Reschedule Marijuana, and Why It's Unlikely Anytime Soon," *Fixgov—Making Government Work* (blog), February 13, 2015 (www.brookings.edu/blogs/fixgov/posts/2015/02/13-how-to -reschedule-marijuana-hudak-wallack), and Hudak and Wallack, "Ending the U.S. Government's War on Medical Marijuana Research," research paper, October 20, 2015 (www.brookings.edu/~ /media/research/files/papers/2015/10/20-war-on-marijuana -research-hudak-wallack/ending-the-us-governments-war-on -medical-marijuana-research.pdf; both accessed May 18, 2016).

5. See Controlled Substances Act, Sections 201(2)(b) and 201(c).

6. Ibid., Section 201(2)(b).

7. The actual vehicle by which a drug is rescheduled by the executive branch comes through the regulatory process and thus is a regulation itself.

8. A report produced by the Drug Policy Alliance that details the trajectory of each marijuana rescheduling petition is an essential resource for the study of administrative rulings on drug policies in the United States. Much of the discussion in this section is based on that report. See Drug Policy Alliance, "The DEA: Four Decades of Impeding and Rejecting Science" (www .drugpolicy.org/sites/default/files/DPA-MAPS_DEA_Science _Final.pdf; accessed May 18, 2016).

9. Ibid., p. 8.

10. Janet E. Joy, Stanley J. Watson, Jr., and John A Benson, Jr., eds., "Marijuana and Medicine: Assessing the Science Base," report prepared for the Institute of Medicine, Division of Neuroscience and Behavioral Health (Washington: National Academy Press and Institute of Medicine, 1999 [http://medicalmarijuana .procon.org/sourcefiles/IOM_Report.pdf; accessed May 18, 2016]).

11. Ibid., pp. 4, 174.

12. Hudak and Wallack, "Ending the U.S. Government's War on Medical Marijuana Research"; Drug Policy Alliance, "The DEA: Four Decades of Impeding and Rejecting Science" (www .drugpolicy.org/sites/default/files/DPA-MAPS_DEA_Science_Final .pdf); Joy, Watson, and Benson, "Marijuana and Medicine."

Chapter Eleven

1. Lee, *Smoke Signals*, pp. 241–42.

2. Bill Clinton, "The President's Radio Address," October 11, 1997 (www.presidency.ucsb.edu/ws/index.php?pid=53393).

3. Lee, *Smoke Signals*, p. 252.

4. "The Administration's response to the passage of California's Proposition 215 and Arizona's Proposition 200." 30 December 1996. Barry McCaffrey: The Office of National Drug Control Policy.

5. By the time of the ruling, the case was called *Conant v. Walters* because the lawsuit extended into the next administration and George W. Bush named John Walters to be drug czar.

6. The CBD oil-only states are Alabama, Florida, Georgia, Iowa, Kentucky, Mississippi, Missouri, North Carolina, Oklahoma, South Carolina, Tennessee, Texas, Utah, Virginia, Wisconsin, and Wyoming.

Chapter Twelve

1. American Civil Liberties Union, "The War on Marijuana in Black and White," June 2013 (www.aclu.org/files/assets/aclu -thewaronmarijuana-rel2.pdf; accessed May 18, 2016).

2. Andrew Golub, Bruce D. Johnson, and Eloise Dunlap, "The Race/Ethnicity Disparity in Misdemeanor Marijuana Arrests in New York City," *Criminology and Public Policy* 6, no. 1 (2007), pp. 131–64.

3. Ricardo Bacca, "Annual Colorado Marijuana Sales Near $900 Million Mark in November," The Cannabist (website), January 13, 2016 (www.thecannabist.co/2016/01/13/colorado -marijuana-sales-taxes-november-2015/46522/).

4. See "U.S. Legalization of Marijuana Has Hit Cartels' Cross-Border Trade," *Time,* April 8, 2015.

5. The Medical Marijuana Enforcement Division was created in 2010 in an effort to enhance the regulatory structure for medical marijuana. In 2013, it was folded into the new Marijuana Enforcement Division.

6. *Printz v. United States* (521 U.S. 898).

7. For a discussion of the events surrounding the exchange between the states and the federal government, see David Blake and Jack Finlaw, "Marijuana Legalization in Colorado: Learned Lessons," *Harvard Law & Policy Review* 8, no. 2 (2014), pp. 359–380 (http://harvardlpr.com/wp-content/uploads/2014/08/HLP204 .pdf).

Chapter Thirteen

1. The first four states to approve recreational marijuana use their alcohol regulatory body to oversee the marijuana program.

2. Miles K. Light and others, "Market Size and Demand for Marijuana in Colorado," report prepared for the Colorado Department of Revenue by the Marijuana Policy Group (www.colorado .gov/pacific/sites/default/files/Market%20Size%20and%20

Demand%20Study,%20July%209,%202014%5B1%5D.pdf; accessed May 18, 2016).

3. Robert A. Mikos, "Marijuana Localism," *Case Western Reserve Law Review* 65, no. 3 (2015), pp. 719–67.

4. John J. Hudak, "Colorado's Rollout of Legal Marijuana Is Succeeding," research paper, Brookings Institution, July 2014 (www.brookings.edu/~/media/research/files/papers/2014/07/colorado-marijuana-legalization-succeeding/cepmmjcov2.pdf; accessed May 1, 2016).

5. Philip A. Wallach, "Washington's Marijuana Legalization Grows Knowledge, Not Just Pot," report, Brookings Institution, August 25, 2014 (www.brookings.edu/research/reports/2014/08/25-washington-marijuana-legalization-knowledge-experiment-wallach; accessed May 18, 2016).

6. Ibid., p. 128.

7. Eric Gorsky, "Colorado Begins Mandatory Testing of Edible Marijuana Potency," *Denver Post,* May 2, 2014 (www.denverpost.com/news/ci_25680313/colorado-begins-mandatory-testing-edible-marijuana-potency).

8. Ibid.

9. There is evidence that racial disparities still exist in marijuana arrests. This suggests that although legalization may start the process toward combatting drugs as a locus of racial injustice in law enforcement, more cultural and social transformations are needed to achieve equitable treatment of the races in the criminal justice system.

10. Christopher Ingraham, "After Legalization, Colorado Pot Arrests Plunge," *Washington Post,* March 26, 2015.

11. In addition to the states in the western block, recreational marijuana initiatives will be on ballots in Massachusetts and Maine, in 2016, as well.

INDEX

relationship with the plant—a relationship believed to be at least 5,000 years old. Instead, it focuses on marijuana policy in the United States. Although at one time unregulated, openly used, and readily prescribed by physicians for the treatment of countless conditions, America's experience with marijuana has been rocky, evolving, and unpredictable. Today, marijuana and the public policy issues it raises are more important than ever.

As of summer 2016, twenty-five states and the District of Columbia had legalized marijuana for medical use. Four states and the District of Columbia had legalized marijuana for recreational use. Numerous states, counties, and municipalities had decriminalized marijuana and its derivatives. Every year legislative proposals are filed in the U.S. Congress that engage the issue. Marijuana's changing policy space has even gained responses from federal courts, the White House, the Department of Justice, the Department of Health and Human Services, and the U.S. Treasury.

New state-level ballot initiatives to legalize the use of marijuana are launched every year, and legalization proposals have and will continue to produce serious debates on the floors of state legislatures. Legalized medical and recreational marijuana are certain to be part of America's future, and so it is essential to understand the history of marijuana policy in the United States.

Marijuana: A Short History offers readers a concise background on marijuana policy in the United States, but without a dry discussion of acts of Congress, Supreme Court rulings, federal agency directives, and treaties—although each will be mentioned. Instead, this book discusses a policy movement more than a century in the

INTRODUCTION

MARIJUANA IS NOT NEW. For millennia, humans have used the cannabis plant for medicine, recreation, religious purposes, and food. The fibers of some cannabis plants, also called hemp, have been used to make rope and textiles. The drug that is made from the plant has also led to the expansion of government power, the imprisonment of hundreds of thousands of individuals, wars waged between nations, and the vilification of some racial and ethnic groups.

Now marijuana has gone mainstream, becoming a relevant part of American public policy debates. Medical and recreational use of marijuana has become an increasingly legitimate and accepted practice in the United States and other nations.

Marijuana has had a long and storied past. This short history is not an exhaustive account of humankind's

MARIJUANA A SHORT HISTORY

Finally, a special note of gratitude goes to my wife, Emily Parsons. Em is a woman with unending patience, listening to me drone on endlessly about pot for months and now years. Her motivation and encouragement through this project—like all projects—have ensured that I am nearly as proud of this book as I am of her each day. She deserves both my love and gratitude.

Christine Jacobs, Dylan Jennings, Ellie Klein, Curtlyn Kramer, Nick McClellan, Cody Poplin, Camilo Ramirez, Liz Sablich, Beth Stone, Strobe Talbott, Liz Thom, and Nick Zeppos. Each deserves my thanks.

Outside of Brookings, a number of people—too many to list completely—have been hugely influential and helpful to me. They include Barb Brohl, Jonathan Caulkins, Mike Collins, Beth Collins and Pat Collins and their daughter, Jennifer Collins, Michael Correia, Sean Easter, Brian Faughnan, Steve Fox, Andrew Freedman, Alison Holcomb, Jeff Kahn, Ron Kammerzell, Beau Kilmer, Mark Kleiman, Blake Komar, Lewis Koski, Miles Light, Stephanie Phillips, Dan Riffle, Kevin Sabet, Steph Sherer, Sue Sisley, Sarah Trumble, John Walsh, and Jeff Zinsmeister.

In addition, I would like to thank my colleagues Bill Brown, Rob Lang, and the entire Brookings Mountain West and UNLV community, as well as, Congressman Earl Blumenauer, and my favorite Nevada state senators, Patricia Farley and Tick Segerblom.

Finally, to all the elected officials, law enforcement, doctors, scientists, activists (on both sides), academics, growers, dispensary owners, marijuana industry employees, and regulators, a huge thank you for opening your doors and letting me in to see exactly what the cannabis world looks like from your point of view. The many people involved in this policy space whom I have visited in Alaska, California, Colorado, Connecticut, the District of Columbia, Nevada, Ohio, and Washington—thank you for your generous offer of time and insight.

A huge thank you goes to the Brookings Institution Press, especially Bill Finan, Valentina Kalk, Janet Walker, and Carrie Engel.

That spurred an interest in marijuana policy of all types and led to extensive research, many trips and interviews, as well as a nearly obsessive reading into the plant, its products, the people, and the policy. Along the way, I worked with a tremendous group of individuals who approach this issue from all directions—from the full-throated advocate to the staunchest of opponents and everyone in between. Their support, guidance, knowledge, experience, personal stories, and perspectives have helped inform my understanding of marijuana policy and made *Marijuana: A Short History* what it is.

Chief among all of the people with whom I have worked is my former colleague and frequent coauthor, Grace Wallack. Grace has an incredible mind for whatever endeavor she undertakes. As in my case, marijuana policy was not a lifelong passion or expected part of her job, but as a team we picked apart some of the most complex issues surrounding marijuana policy and sought to explain them to whomever would listen. It turned out, a lot of people listened. Without her support, intellect, motivation, and ability to keep me on track, the marijuana research emerging from my office would have been a shell of what it is today. She deserves both the highest of praise and my complete gratitude.

Other Brookings colleagues have helped inform my work, my understanding of marijuana policy, and were excellent sounding boards as this book came to fruition. Phil Wallach, Jon Rauch, Ashley Gabriele, the Brookings Creative Lab Team (George Burroughs, Sareen Hairabedian, Mark Hoelscher, Zach Kulzer, Ian McAllister), Ashley Bennett, Jessica Brandt, Bob Brier, Brittany Brown-Hart, Stephanie Dahle, Courtney Dunakin, Anna Goodbaum,

ACKNOWLEDGMENTS

WORKING ON MARIJUANA reform was one of the last things I expected would be part of my career when I began doing political and policy research. I am not an advocate; I am a political scientist. I was not trained in the study of drug policy; I was trained in the study of political institutions, specifically the presidency and the bureaucracy.

However, sometimes very interesting opportunities fall into your lap, and a new venture becomes a career highlight. Marijuana policy is exactly that. I came to this issue in part by happenstance and largely because a colleague of mine, Jonathan Rauch, encouraged me to ask the types of questions my research focuses on (regulation, personnel, bureaucratic organization, and executive-legislative interaction) and apply it to a new and emerging area of policy: the legalization of adult-use marijuana.

CONTENTS

For Michelle Dean

Copyright © 2016
THE BROOKINGS INSTITUTION
1775 Massachusetts Avenue, N.W., Washington, D.C. 20036
www.brookings.edu

Library of Congress Cataloging-in-Publication data are available.
ISBN 9-780-8157-2906-8 (pbk : alk. paper)
ISBN 9-780-8157-2907-5 (ebook)
9 8 7 6 5 4 3 2 1

Typeset in Sabon

Composition by Westchester Publishing Services

MARIJUANA

John Hudak

BROOKINGS INSTITUTION PRESS
Washington, D.C.